TO SAVE THE WORLD

TO SAVE THE WORLD

THERE IS NO "SANTA CLAUS"!

T HANS

AUCTOREM
HOUSE

Auctorem House
276 5th Ave, Ste 704-2591
New York, NY 10001
www.auctoremhouse.com
Phone: 1 888-332-7718

Published by Auctorem House: 11/13/2024

ISBN: 978-1-965687-12-3(sc)
ISBN: 978-1-965687-13-0(e)

Library of Congress Control Number: 2024920019

Contents

"Yes!" To My Sylvie

It seems like ages ago –

March 15, 2023 – and I was sitting in front of my computer... probably thinking about our United Family. It was a normal day for me. But then my telephone rang. My phone is right next to my computer so it was easy to answer it with – "This is Hans! A nice voice came from "the other end" asking... "Is Sharon there? My quick response was – "There is no Sharon here... you must have the wrong number. Who are you looking for?" The friendly voice replied, "I am looking for this author, since I am in marketing for a publishing company. Is there any chance you are an author? Have you done any writing?" I said something like, "I have done some writing a long time ago – I wrote four ebooks that are still available on Amazon's Kindle Select, T. Hans Olson, author.

Slowly, I began to realize we had a lot we could talk about... so I added, "My latest book is titled, "To Save The World – There Is No "Santa Claus"! "Wow!" (or something like it) I heard from the very nice female voice. I found out the person I was chatting with over the telephone was named Sylvie Montero -- a marketing agent in charge of finding authors. It was an almost immediate connection between us... since I love to talk and since she was "in her element" talking about writing and books. We chatted back and forth with writing thoughts as well as personal information... getting more and more enthusiastic and excited as time moved on. We were having so much fun talking to each other that time just flew by!

I am sure we had nearly an hour of fun conversation, when Sylvie just blurted out... in an excited tone, "Will you marry me?"

Surprised as I could be, I just yelled out to her over the phone --- "YES"!!! We couldn't escape talking about our affectionate words to each other. Yes, we both knew there were true feelings behind our words... and yet there was a need to come back to reality too.

We continued to chat on and on to each other about "who knows what" but there was a bond between us... and later on in the day we spoke to each other again. The "upshot" of this amazing experience for both of us is..... Sylvie and I agreed that in the future, we would want to call this simple, revolutionary book "our baby"...

With love....Sylvie and Hans

Introduction

You might get surprised if you look into this book and start reading. I'm guessing that you won't ever think the same way again after you finish reading these 54 pages – that is, if you really finish reading it all! Some people will be flabbergasted and just shake their heads. Some people will deny, deny, deny and then be concerned. Some people will be angry and upset. Some people will almost collapse with grief. Some people will feel sorry for the author. Some people will want to kill the author. Some people will feel threatened. Some people will feel that they have lost their calling. Some people will be confused and bewildered. Some people will feel as though they have been thrown under the bus. Some people will have some questions and want to talk about it. Some people will begin to understand. Some people will applaud vigorously. Some people will want to change almost everything. Some people will say, "Bravo, I told you so!" There will be many and more reactions, if people study these pages. Probably every person will react differently. But no one will ever think the same way again.

So here's part of the title: To save the world. There's a lot of talk about being saved or getting saved these days. Are you saved? Jesus saves! Who will be saved? Of course, comments or questions like these refer almost totally to personal salvation. A lot of religious people want to get others changed for the better and saved for another life. It's becoming clearer these days that the most dominant force bringing about change in the world is humanity – for better and for worse. According to our best scientific research, in the very earliest period of the world's existence, evolution was probably the most important change agent. Then there could have been a moment in history when a cosmic force changed or threatened the world's future. Obviously, such impacts on the world occurred over vast periods of time. Fast forward to the world as we know it and we are beginning to realize that there are events that could take place which would significantly alter life on our planet very quickly. For example, a release of explosive military power around the world could bring human existence to basic subsistence or an incremental deterioration and complete annihilation. This probably could happen as quickly as some cosmic intervention. Then there is the impact the human species has had on all the rest of living things, say nothing about the effect our present day lifestyle has had on our environment. Over the history of the world, such changes are happening so quickly they can be envisioned as if a moment in a human life. The world seems to be getting more vulnerable to sickness, deterioration and death. Actually most of us think that a lot needs to be changed in the world, and yes, saved. Why should we be concerned about the world? Why shouldn't we just do what we want to do and can do and let the chips fall where they may? Wouldn't it be acceptable to just do what needs to be done on a daily basis and let the world fend for itself? Such a philosophy would be a lot less troublesome than thinking we have the responsibility or the capability of changing the direction the world is heading. How different would that be than what we are doing now – just hoping to make sure we have a personal existence beyond this world? We are led to believe that personal salvation is what we should be concerned about – isn't that what's most important? In our present day and age, we are encouraged to look out for ourselves. Let future generations take care of themselves. There's not too much of a problem with this other than to realize we may be faulted for causing future damage or destruction. In the history of the world, would we like to be compared to the force that killed the dinosaurs? How can we deal with that? Maybe it's best to brush such thoughts away and take care of our own problems.

Now there are some people who might be a bit concerned about... what our children and grandchildren might be facing in the future... what might be causing us some problems in the present... what obviously is happening to many of the world's living things right now... and what responsibilities we might have for what we are doing to ourselves. Should such people be simply pushed aside, ignored or banned to some distant, unseen place? That shouldn't be too hard to do, especially if the majority rules. Concerned people certainly aren't very influential or powerful in today's world. So the dominant theme should be to carry on, and life should be able to go on without too much fuss. Done.

But wait a minute. What does it mean to save the world? Wouldn't the world still exist if it wasn't saved? Obviously, one needs to ascertain some limits between a saved world and one that is not saved. Where does one begin? Some species have already gone out of existence – have not been saved. Others are hanging on by a thread – they need some kind of rescue in order to be saved. Probably the readers of this book are most concerned about the survival of the human species. If humanity could survive on the planet with some minimal contentment, chances are that quite a few others could also. But mere survival on our planet wouldn't mean very much if there wasn't a happy / meaningful / promising, etc. quality of life. What might be a level of deterioration beyond which humanity would no longer want to live on the earth? If the earth could be held to certain minimal standards, which are acceptable to a majority of the earth's human population, maybe such a level or better could be understood as a saved world.

It seems quite clear that the world has deteriorated in recent years. Certain birds, animals and plant life have died out. For them the world has not been saved. What is essential to a good life? Here are a few basic needs: adequate (quality or uncontaminated) sunshine, water, air, food, shelter, living space, fertile soil, energy resources, physical protection, propagation stimulation... and there are probably many more basics. Without any one of these, human life may not be able to survive. When one begins to seriously think about it, the world is a pretty delicate, fragile, vulnerable place for enjoyable living, and it wouldn't seem to take much imbalance to ruin or destroy it. We also know already that human population increase on the planet has become a major factor in our overall happiness and contentment. When human beings fight with one another because they live in constant fear for their lives, when most people no longer can attain adequate supplies of food or water, when there is an obvious threat to personal survival or the survival of one's children, when irritations become so great that life no longer seems worth living, when individuals feel dominated or cornered to the point that they lash out with little fear, when these or other threats to living on our planet become pressing or personal, clearly, overall human existence becomes very vulnerable. Thinking about some of the above threats, are we presently living in a time when we are beginning to see a series of basic building blocks falling apart and chaos reigning? Will there come a point in the near future when our ingenuity or creativity will no longer have a chance to save the world because too much damage has been done? If so, do we still have the time, the will or the resources to stop the deterioration and try to save the world? If we are a hopeful, powerful and perceptive people, it's possible that there is still time to do what's necessary for the survival of our species and the remaining parts of our planet.

At this time there is no political or religious debate as to who and/or what will save the world. Could it be that we as humans are so caught-up with our own salvation, due to the drift / momentum of religious teachings over the last couple of thousand years, that we can't and don't want to think about the larger world in which we live? How sad, when one thinks about this, that our egotistical and selfish ideas and theological precepts have blinded us to what is fundamental or essential to our basic survival as a human race – a world many of us originally believed was beautifully created for joy and happiness. I would guess that as long as we cling desperately to our personal salvation mentality and our man-made arguments concerning our most important place in the world, we will essentially destroy ourselves and our source of life and breath. Another question: Have religions in general encouraged what has led us toward the destruction of our planet – the egocentric desire for the perfect life beyond the world in which we live? If we can escape our lives here and live in a better place, why should we be concerned about saving what is in front of us now? How does the reality of scientific study speak to this way of thinking? Is God really a gray-hair old man up in the sky that wants to have each of us pampered in some faraway place for eternity? Who are our sports heroes pointing to when they gesture to the sky after making their grand show of accomplishment? But can we as individuals give up our fanciful thoughts of winning the lottery at the time of our death? Sadly, that might be as unlikely as saving the world.

In some sense, I tremble a bit inside as I compose these words that are going down in black and white. Here's a discussion about personal salvation, saving the world and then the title comment that there is no Santa Claus. What could these words mean to millions of people who have fully tossed themselves into their belief system and way of life? Would it be too cruel to lay it out that there is no Santa Claus? You were little once and you believed what you were told... especially by mom and dad. It's hard not to accept grown-up thinking at a young age, when everything you see around you seems so fun and beautiful and comfortable. Just let sleeping dogs lie, as the saying goes. Isn't there plenty of time down the road to see the whole world honestly in the overwhelming light of day? So when is the proper time to come clean and get started on the tough tasks ahead? But I'm getting ahead of myself. Santa Claus is just for children, right? And there are countless adults ready and willing to keep the little children in the dark as long as possible. In fact, many of those adults make a good profit from the ignorance of children. Chalk it all up to the way things have been done in the past. As the thinking goes, "If it has been good enough for me, it should be good enough for a lot of other people."

If everything was peaceful and under control in our world, there might not need to be any re-evaluation of human thinking and planning. But in just the last few decades, human beings have made some big changes. These changes have seriously affected, altered and deteriorated our relationships and surroundings. The future doesn't look very bright for the next generation... even in the near future. What will happen if there is even more separation between the rich and the poor? Will the climate and weather patterns continue to become even more chaotic... making life miserable for a good share of the world's population? Even political differences give rise to uncooperative and even violent actions. Are different cultures and races coming more into conflict? The priorities of various nations seem to be headed further and further apart as relations between them get tense and problematic. Questions and concerns like these make us more than a little worried. Just as a serious illness for a man or woman can seemingly jeopardize one's entire outlook on life, so the world seems to be getting less healthy, sicker and has an increasing need for emergency action. All this is initiating more than a little reason for concern.

How did the world get sick and start to lose its life, health and ability to function normally? As is the case with most illnesses, the first signs of instability or problematic symptoms are usually cast aside or ignored. Who wants to change direction when most of the signs ahead say "go"... and almost everyone is headed in that same direction? Yes, the first indications of the world's weaknesses started many centuries back in time and were certainly unrecognized.

If we are looking for answers about saving the world, there are plenty of arguments about which side is correct on the political spectrum and also about who has the right religion. Each issue that comes up seems rather complex and many believe each position is just a matter of personal preference. One might conclude there are no answers to the complexity of life these days. So the miss-mash of ideas and solutions offer a declining and deteriorating world with less and less possibilities. I believe that there are better and worse solutions (as one looks at religion and politics) and that there are good and bad answers to the problems that face our planet and the human race.

Has anyone seriously thought about our human

responsibility to save the world? Granted that apparently a gigantic impact from space wiped the dinosaurs (and many other forms of life) off the planet a long time ago. So should we rely purely on this kind of accidental bad luck or good luck as to whether or not the earth survives for human habitation in the future? What if something humans do or don't do affects whether humans can or cannot survive on earth? So far, it appears that human beings have left our future to the trite phrase, "whatever happens, happens!" The other strong possibility is that mankind has left the future of the world all up to god or a mysterious religious phenomenon. How about that for a way to get us all off the hook and let us either escape or overlook the mess we've created?

Is it too early or too late to talk about saving the world? Is there any advantage one way or the other? What are the implications of not doing anything about such a question? Or maybe the question is beyond the scope of human understanding, ambition, contemplation or activity!? With this question we are dealing with the environment, home, source of happiness, future and reality of every human being. With this question, we deal with something everyone can have partnership with – unlike contemplating personal salvation, which no person can control. Shouldn't the earth's inhabitants have something to say about the sustainability, durability, future, quality, condition… of their own home? What if the human race has nothing to say or do about whether the world is saved or not? What if we started out with imagining that we are not saved for an after-life? What would be the consequences? How is one to know? But now imagine our present world with no extended life. There are all kinds of things that could go wrong in the immediate future, say nothing about an extended one. What should be our most serious / urgent / important / personal / corporate concern?

To get a bit of a handle on all of this, it would be good to try to learn what is needed for a person to be happy and fulfilled on this earth. For everyone to be happy, fulfilled and hopeful, it's critical that we get straightened out what humanity needs and what is enough. Then there could be a coming together of those who have too much and those who have too little. The world has existed with a delicate balance in our environment. It has provided what we have needed to develop, grow and flourish as individuals, families, communities and nations. What happens when things get "out of balance"? Unimaginable consequences almost certainly develop. That's what's happening today around the world. We have not carried out the proper steps to maintain "balance" in our lives, communities and nations. When will we come to understanding the fact that we need to take some serious steps to save the world? Will it be too late? Will all hell break loose? Are we approaching that point in our world today? We need to become aware of our situation before we can do something to correct the imbalances. This book might give us a little nudge in that direction.

Yes, the world is big, but is the world too big to deal with? Are we each too small to have an impact on the world's condition? Will the world be different because of an individual's existence? Where do we go from here? There needs to be some thinking that goes into what's ahead and what can be done. Decisions are being made moment by moment by each and every person. Those decisions will have a small but vital impact on the future of our world. Will we (as human beings) have an impact on our personal and corporate destination down the road? The answer is a definite, "Yes."

The responsible and grown up position for us as intelligent human beings is that we should hold ourselves responsible for the condition of the world. After all, we have been the dominant and most prolific species the world has known for as long as there has been a record of human existence. If there is to be a future accidental tragedy that strikes our planet, we should try to minimize the damage and restore whatever measure of health we can to the earth. If the deterioration of the world is caused by human ignorance or misdeeds, we should not be thinking we can simply leave the mess we have created to future generations, or even worse, to a lonely, forsaken, deteriorating and dying planet. We

can do better. It's in our own interest, as caretakers of
the earth, to save the world.

So let's get started on the treacherous task ahead. There's
no question that the goal of saving the world is a rather
large and challenging one.

The Problem

A look at a familiar tune should give us a little indication of what has been going on for a long, long time in our society. The words in these four short, catchy verses lay out clearly how we have handled the Christmas celebration – an exciting, fun, special, profitable, rewarding and thoughtful time at the end of every year. Who hasn't gotten carried away with all this at some point in their lives? Take a look at the words...

Santa Claus is Coming to Town

You better watch out
You better not cry
Better not pout
I'm telling you why
Santa Claus is coming to town

He's making a list
And checking it twice
Gonna find out Who's naughty and nice Santa Claus
is coming to town

He sees you when you're sleeping
He knows when you're awake
He knows if you've been bad or good
So be good for goodness sake!

O! You better watch out!
You better not cry
Better not pout
I'm telling you why
Santa Claus is coming to town
Santa Claus is coming to town

(The words of this Christmas song were written by John Frederick Coots and Haven Gillespie. It was first sung on Eddie Cantor's radio show in November 1934.)

Most of us have heard of this song very early in life and many have had it memorized. As little children we were told about Santa and he was an important part of our Christmas celebrations, especially when we were very little. Now, consider the familiar words of this song as an adult. If you were a little child, wouldn't these verses almost put the fear of God into you? Santa Claus knows all about you and he's keeping track of your goodness and/or badness. Be good and you will be rewarded when he arrives! Yes, Santa has some leverage. Parents like to use leverage too!

If your child or children believed in Santa Claus at some point in their young lives, when was the right time to tell the truth? The more convincing the story and the longer the tale was believed, the more difficult it was or would be to straighten out the truth of the matter. Now, here comes the tough part. What if you were told that there is no keeping track of your goodness and/or badness from the ultimate point of view? What if you were told today, as an adult, that there is no reward or punishment after you die? What if you were told that there is no Santa Claus? Would you be crushed? Would your whole world collapse around you? Would your morality be lost or forsaken? For many religious people around the world – who have been led to believe that if they just do and believe the right things they will be rewarded with eternal life – those religious people will most likely have their whole view of the world turned upside down. Just think of today's terrorists who give away their lives in order to get all those rewards in heaven. Around the world, countless people do terrible things because of their beliefs. The brainwashing they receive in their religious Santology is simply used as leverage to get them to do extremely foolish or stupid things. How sad (and some may say evil) to string along these desperate people. True, it should be acknowledged that the people who believe in such nonsense are not thinking very clearly and are not doing much to compare fantasy with reality. But let's be honest: Almost all of us trust our authority figures (including parents) to play it straight in our serious discussions. We have believed what we've been told... in spite of all evidence to the contrary.

So here are some questions worth thinking about regarding Santa stories as well as religious brainwashing. How many parents would want their children to continue to believe in Santa Claus as they grow older? How many parents believe their children would live better lives carrying along the story of Santa? Is there anything lost in living our daily lives while believing such stories? What is downright detrimental in living in such a fantasy land? How do religious stories from the ancient past compare with our Santa stories today? Who needs rewards from Santa to live good, productive, happy lives? Why do we need to be with loved ones after we die? And finally, what are the benefits of being told all these tall tales other than to keep us from growing up?

It might be good to begin to reassess our ideas about personal salvation. What should be our point of emphasis as we live out our daily lives? Should we be trying to do what needs to be done to reassure ourselves that we will get a place in heaven, or should we be actually living our lives in a way that is necessary to save the world for ourselves and others? It's the difference between living with a "Santa Claus" mentality or dream – if we are good enough we'll get rewarded down the road (depending upon some god to get us what we want in some future state) – and living in the moment...thinking and acting to do something concretely for our present and future happiness. Is it time for us to grow up rather than to push away our present responsibilities to live in dreamland? Of course, who wants to have their fairyland removed after believing in it so earnestly and for so long? The political stance is to ignore, postpone, deny and argue for present convenience, laziness and irresponsibility.

It's a fact that we are for the most part a greedy and relatively thankless society. Who among us doesn't want "more"? Why are the lotteries so popular? If we were truly satisfied, we would be very thankful for what we have and we would be speaking up and working to help others receive enough. Instead, we complain about the wasteful poor or the convicts who are having it too nice. We complain about what we have to pay in taxes, as though we weren't getting our fair share. Being the most wealthy and powerful nation ever on the face of the globe, we can't get enough resources from the outside world. We have little desire to cut back on our standard of living in order to see that other nations catch up with better living conditions. So we have little time to feel or say thank you for the little things which we should be enjoying in our daily lives.

When there are few significant thank yous, society, community and family simply become more proficient in thoughtlessness and greed. When was the last time you received a thank you for something nice that you did, or for something you made, or for a compliment, or for just being gracious? People are generally so into themselves that they seem to have little time to express their appreciation. Of course, there are exceptions to the rule, but the dominant sentiments are what carry the day. Where should people be learning thankfulness? When have we (you and I) received enough? And who in this interdependent world should be on the receiving end? Was there something to the comment Jesus made when he said, "As you have done it to one of the least of these (my brothers and sisters), you have done it unto me."?

Consider the options if we really do want to become more mature. Think about what happens when what we have treasured in our minds and hearts goes down the drain? Well, all is not lost! In fact, the way, the truth and the life sets us free, believe it or not! That's the conclusion of today's scientific analysis. Let's carefully work our way toward this liberating reality.

I would guess that almost all religions have laid out requirements for their faithful followers. Who in the world has laid out these theologies? You can be certain that through the ages important men have done the dirty work – not only ancient men who have been popular with their contemporaries, but also men who have decided to convince people to toe the line. (Of course, they haven't thought of their suggestions as dirty work.) Now if a person wants others to do their bidding, that person better have some leverage. How about something that can never be proven true or false? That will make people think. Since most people are motivated by the carrot and the stick, how about heaven and hell? No matter how you feel about these two motivators, you have to admit that if you bring up the subject, you can get a lot of people thinking about what's going to happen to them after they die. And who doesn't want the afterlife to be a pleasant experience? That's especially true for people who have nothing going for them in their present lives – probably most of those people who sacrifice themselves to blow up others. These are very vulnerable and ignorant people being led down a very dark path just for the chance to have a wonderful eternity. There is motivation and leverage aplenty! The power of popular leaders who use fantasy religious stories to get followers is downright awesome among those who are desperate, angry, ignorant, cheated and very susceptible to all kinds of lies. You get the picture, right? There aren't many of us who would be against letting those confused and ignorant little people know that there is no Santa Claus.

But we need to move on. The number of people who are captivated to become terrorists is a relatively small number considering the world's population. What about the vast majority of the world's people who are faithfully trying to carry out the fundamentals of the world's religions? How could so many people get caught up in the search of a hoped for future? How could promises, promises as well as vulnerability to an unknown future motivate everyone to reach for the stars? How does the religious establishment hold on to the wishful, point to heaven crowd? The answers are a bit mind-boggling.

Here's a sampling of the reasons religions still seem to be the only game in town. In a nation of rich abundance, consider how many people irrationally gamble their money away as well as try to win the lottery? Could that be more than a few wishful thinkers and insecure money managers? That's a Santa Claus mentality and religions do their best to cash in. You can have it all... when you die. In a country where the military establishment and patriotic zeal is out of this world, and where extensive U.S. military hardware is for sale around the world, and where Americans feel threatened inside and outside our borders, and where there seems to be a threatening agent around every corner – where all this is happening on an daily and hourly basis (and this may well be judged the most secure nation on earth), consider how fragile, insecure, vulnerable and susceptible the nations of the world are in these troubled times. Does this provide an opening for the religious fast talkers? Are people generally looking for some outside source of security and earnestly seeking the Santa Claus story? You bet they are.

There are many more examples of why countless people are caught up with wishful thinking about life after death. Who isn't looking for fun and games these days? Even in the remote areas of the world, men, women and children swarm to parties, entertaining events, television sets and just wild spectacles to escape the mundane activities of their routine lives. In addition there are the drugs and physical manipulators that many go after in order to get away. All of this advertises escape to a better place. Consequently, the masses are very open to suggestions that "Santa Claus is coming to town" after they die. What an easy sell to people who want it all – if not now, then for eternity. There are plenty of salesmen and now saleswomen who can make a good pitch for heaven... of course including whatever one might want with them to feel happy.

Seduction is the word that can explain our human vulnerability these days. How about selling the importance of self, a me first mentality and the ultimate value of every human life? Now it's true that good self-esteem is a valuable character trait for a healthy human existence. But what does egocentric thinking cost the rest of the creation? This infantile me mentality has to do with selfish accumulation and fighting for power over others. This is an easy pitch for how much God wants every individual to be with him forever, while being entertained with all the best of fantasy living. Everlasting life sounds very good to a self-absorbed person. The big ego can shove everything else aside as that person lives out life on our planet looking to cash in sometime in the future. A final example of how easy it is to promote the rewards of religion is that human beings are not only creatures of habit but also have deep roots in their traditions and biological makeup. To put it simply, there's a great incentive to go along with the crowd, to do what seems to have worked in the past and to listen to those who are theoretically the experts. Consider the enormous leverage we give to religions and to the authority of their leaders as time flows on and everyone seems to be sucked along. Who can argue (at any point in history) that there are ultimately no rewards and punishments for human beings, that there is no afterlife and that religions are simply nonsense at worst or fascinating stories at best to help us escape the realities of life? Who should ever suggest that there is no Santa Claus and that everything we have been told about life after death is just a big lie to get us to be good for a while? Any takers? Very few, if any. That's a major reason why the religions of the world hold vast power over the human species, even though there are significant risks in continuing to stick to the story.

The significant risks (of sticking to the story) are pretty scary, when a person starts to think about it. Let's look at a few. Religions command a lot of attention and resources from their followers. What religions demand, require or ask for can't be used elsewhere. Now granted that religions have done a lot of good things over the centuries. They have kept spirits high even in the midst of difficult times, they have often provided guidance for critical choices, they have offered people a group of friends for satisfying and uplifting activities, they have usually taught basic, sturdy morals for healthy living and they have provided many social services that have been very helpful in developing countries. What's not to like? Still, looking over this list of commendable benefits, are there any that couldn't be provided by a good social club? Of course, some religious groups are not much more than social clubs. But now, to get back to the point, think about what religions have absorbed or have deflected from other points of vital interest. The amount of money that has been absorbed in the name of the so called spiritual life is almost unimaginable. Consider what the religious leadership has used for its own personal purposes, what the worship centers have cost in time, talents and money, the time, emotional feelings and spiritual support that followers have donated, the time taken for teaching, developing and repeating the story line, the promotion of particular religious perspectives in larger communities and cities – these and still other aspects of the so called spiritual life have been absorbed or used up over the centuries... for what? The big focus has always been eternal life.

Religions have looked at our total human experience with a relatively narrow perspective of the world. It could be said that religions have required a perspective about life on earth (from beginning to end) that has rivaled the current scientific view of the world and even the universe. This is no small invasion into the human perspective of what life has been, what life is in the present and even what life should be like in the future. There has been a wrestling among religions and even with the scientific community about the real story about human existence and human experience. This contention or difference of opinion has slipped into human thinking about life on earth, about meaning in the human experience and even about life and death matters. As long as humanity is torn within between the emotional fantasy or the realities of life on earth, the cost of this struggle is gigantic and even now has required a very high cost to our house and home. How long should religions hold power over the masses as their stories, pronouncements and requests continue to cost the human family its very sustenance?

Maybe it's a telling scenario that the political party in the U.S. which theoretically claims the conservative Christian outlook in 2016 is supporting the biggest ego ever in the history of candidates running for President of the United States. Certainly this is a sign of the times as well as a sign of the grossness and illegitimacy of today's Christian thinking and activity. Where Jesus

Christ was cast as the humble servant and as the most sacrificial example of a human being, today's leader of religious fundamentalism and political power is a man of ignorance, rash judgments, self-promotion, aggression, greed, pride and arrogance. His theme is to make "America great again", as though America doesn't already have many times more material wealth and defensive power than any nation in the history of the world. His answers (for the future greatness of this country) are to shut people out, ridicule and stomp on the opposition and promote the use of guns in the U.S. What kind of Christian example is this to the world? Yes, religious hypocrisy runs rampant in today's world, yet the ignorant masses hold on to their "visions of sugar plums"... coming on that dying day when their all-knowing savior/Santa offers the good children (or believing children) more fun and games. Here's the religious answer to the world's problems: How about doing more Christmas shopping so that the economy can be increased for the emotional fantasy lovers who already have too much? Greed is a form of violence which counteracts peace and love – two commodities in short supply. We have a sick society, to be sure.

In these days before electing our next president, upheaval seems to be everywhere. The daily news is filled with discussion about revolt from both the right and the left. Donald Trump has introduced talking points which have many people (especially those in the Right Wing of the Republican Party) expressing extreme unhappiness with the political establishment in Washington. Trump has en-flamed many people's fears and prejudices, seems to have a great number of followers and is causing significant concern about a possible chaotic future for the United States, especially if this troubled man is elected president. Is this an indication of how greedy, selfish, prejudiced, dictatorial, and rebellious we have become in this country? Is Donald Trump expressing the underlying feelings of our nation's citizens, just as the lottery mentality has seemingly captured American hopes and dreams?

Do we have any hope based on reality? We have plenty of problems – climate change, terrorism, major refugee problems, religious divisions, violence, wars, the widening gap between the rich and poor, a me first mentality, a mad race into materialism and nothingness, competition pushing away cooperation, "God is on my side" thinking, as well as the lottery mentality and the sadness it suggests. So where can a person find any hope for a world dominated by religions?

The real truth is that the religions of the world in their pompous proclamations, authoritarian dictates and gaudy extravagances have done a lot of damage to the earth and its inhabitants. Wars have been fought, human beings have dominated, degraded and destroyed much of the world's environment, unimaginable resources have been wasted, some people have been put on pedestals while others have been condemned to stoning (and still others to hell), different religions and even different denominations have gone after one-another tooth and nail, people have been labeled as good or bad with far reaching if not never ending consequences in their daily living, and finally, and maybe most importantly, individuals have given almost everything to find eternal security. They have jumped off the cliff so to speak, all based on theologies from the ancient past that relied on people's imaginations (if not the clever manipulations of emotions) by questionable men intending to secure leverage and obedience. The religions of the world have caused more than a few problems. It's time we grew up and learned the truth. There is no Santa Claus.

The Possibilities

Where does telling the truth about our world leave us? Actually, it moves us a great distance forward in body, mind and spirit. First, let's take the body. One thing that a good share of humanity finds valuable and rewarding is love. A good share of the world's religious traditions focus on love. One thing that the Christian tradition and the New Testament focuses on is the self-giving love of Jesus Christ. We read that God is love. Love and peace are basically what people desire. There's not much that can deny the fact of love in human experience. The love shared between human beings is essential to our very existence. There's no denying it. Love makes the world go around and it keeps us in the midst of fruitful, healthy living. The human body needs love shared between individuals... among family members... and spread into communities, nations and around the world. God is love and love is meant to be shared. In this experience we are talking about the more mature life of supporting and building up others, working together for a united purpose and cooperating with others. Of course the body has its life-time limits, and with feelings of wanting love continued, we would like to have our lives extended to another life. Who can control that extension? No one has that power. It's just wishful thinking. Religion ventured into this void to give us our fantasy. As little children, we soaked up the attention, accepted the requirements and dreamed of the sought after reward. But it all was just child's play and a carefully contrived emotional experience unconnected to real life. So what shall we do learning the truth? Rather than make up stories and play games with one another, why not leave that thinking and daydreaming outside our power altogether? Why not leave the after-life (if there is one) to a simple mystery? That leaves us without any rewards or punishments. That leaves us without being captive to any leverage. That leaves us without that extended ego desiring to go beyond what we know is real. And finally that leaves us able to take care of what's really important in our lives. Rather than work to try to secure our future happiness after death, we can spend our time enhancing the one life we know we have been given.

Imagine a world where the people of the world spend their precious days developing good relationships with others, learning how interdependent all things are in the whole creation, practicing techniques for enhancing and caring for our earthly environment, teaching conservation for the benefit of future generations and finally trusting our best instincts to make the best of what we already have. We leave any future life to mystery, just as we leave the universe and creation to mystery. That gives us freedom from the hard work, mental anguish and unknown consequences of the whole heaven and hell thing. We are given freedom from the law to enjoy grace and truth and reality. There's no more wondering about when we will get the story straightened out. Now we don't have to figure out how to get saved... with all that entails. Now we can learn how to make the best of all we have been given for the days we have in us. We can help our fellow human beings learn how to save the world. In truth, we have been so caught up in getting saved ourselves (in our small egotistical world) that we have lost sight of how important it is to take care of every one of our fellow human beings as well as all parts of the planet which is our home. This is the true reality of our day by day existence. Think about a creator (or something beyond us that creates, saves and is good at change) – wouldn't that mystery god be thrilled (to put it in human terms) that part of the creation is into protecting that original, ongoing, mind-boggling, creation of the world? I think so. Not only that but now we can live more comfortably with the real world and our present scientific endeavor.

Freeing up our bodies for living in the moment has tangible, beneficial rewards. Each religion has left it up to its own particular authority to take care of ultimate justice and whatever happens in the future. Of course, for the most part, those authorities are all different, and in the minds of their leaders, their doctrines and teachings are worth fighting for. With every different story told to every different group of ignorant innocents, you can imagine the confusion and the complexities of everyone on this earth getting along with one another. Religions have not brought people together, they have separated them – emotionally, intellectually and usually physically. This unforeseen reality could be one of the most detrimental consequences of the rise in the power and authority of religions in the world. Is this really true? Are religions essentially causing trouble for continuing human existence on this small planet? It's true. How about that for an ironic twist of fate? Yes, the conflicts in our world today, the confusions between peoples and the basic hatefulness of one group toward another dissimilar group of people, all this should make thoughtful individuals sit up and take notice. The religions of the world are in large part responsible. It would be good to be free of this confusing aspect of our lives.

How about freedom from two bad alternatives? In their religious zeal, some people have pushed themselves forward in their daily lives and have tried to dominate others with their own personal convictions. Still others have retreated from life's struggles and have wasted their potential looking forward to an after-life with hopefully many rewards. Which use of a human life would be more admirable? Honestly, neither position is valuable for enhancing life on our planet. For religious people to try to control others or for them to try to escape into fantasy land is simply bad for our real world, which has endured for a long time with the themes of balance and harmony. To create unnecessary conflict among unnecessary groups for the purpose of advancing unnecessary stories to get fantasy rewards in a fantasy future – all this is a total detriment to a fragile planet. If the original purpose of religions was to help people get along with one another and/or to set up some reward or punishment system to get them to say and do the right things, then over many centuries religions have failed miserably. They should be rejected as severely outdated tools for the healthy development of the world. It's time for human beings to grow up, be told the truth about the world, get clued in on its entire human family, become informed about our mutual responsibilities for one another, be reminded about the fragile nature of the environment in which we live (and what we can and should do to reestablish what we have destroyed) and finally to set our minds on the honest facts about what can be done to save the world as a better home for an extended future. It's way past time that we grew up and face the facts of our limited lives on earth. We can forget about the stories of our childish days as well as about any fantasy future we may have imagined. We can use all we have been given in this life to enjoy it, enhance it, protect it and revel in its goodness for whatever time we have been given. It's time we put away childish things (there is no Santa Claus) and learned to love. For those who have participated in the Christian religion, there's an appropriate and thoughtful chapter in the Bible's New Testament (I Corinthians 13) that goes something like this:

"I may be able to speak the languages of men and even of angels, but if I don't have love, my speech is no more than a noisy gong or clanging bell. I may have the gift of inspired preaching and have all knowledge and understand all secrets. I may have all the faith needed to move mountains, but if I don't have love, it does me no good. I may give away everything I have and even give up my body to be burned, but if I don't have love it does me no good.

Love is patient and kind. It's not jealous or conceited or proud. Love is not ill-mannered, selfish or irritable. Love doesn't keep a record of wrongs. It's not happy with evil but is happy with the truth. Love never gives up. Its faith, hope and patience never fail.

Love is eternal. There are inspired messages but they are partial. There are gifts of speaking but they will cease. There is knowledge, but it will pass. For our gifts of knowledge and inspired messages are only partial, but when what is perfect comes, then what is partial disappears.

When I was a child, my speech, feelings and thinking were all those of a child. When I became a man I gave up childish ways. What we see now is like seeing in the dim image of a mirror. Then we shall see face to face. What I know now is only partial, then it will be complete, as complete as God's knowledge of me. Meanwhile, these three remain – faith, hope and love. But the greatest of these is love."

The above passage is not meant to be taken literally as a final truth. In fact, it even states with its verses that inspired messages are only partial. What is stated in a simple, clear way is that love is what is enduring. That's a truth that's worth holding onto forever. It says, let go of all those childish ways. That's something quite profound for the real world of grownups.

Today, in making good use of our limited time on this planet, each person should clearly be responsible for his or her particular gifts and abilities, as long or as short as that time might be. For every individual, the mature inspiration for words and deeds is the love that reaches out to benefit the whole creation. As a human species we have the ability and power (if used appropriately) to not only preserve the wonderful home we are enjoying but to enhance it or recreate it beyond what presently exists. But we need to focus… not egotistically on our own personal salvation (which essentially we have no control over anyway)… but on saving and preserving our home life for ourselves, our global family, our children and grandchildren as well as for generations in the future. As large a project as that seems to be, each person has the power to affect that earthly reality in the here and now. If we are given a life as a human on this planet, this is our purpose – to live out what we have been given to the best of our ability, as small or as large as that impact on the whole creation might be. This is a wonderful purpose, considering our place in the universe. As each person acts together with other members of his or her earthly family, essentially an everlasting impact can be made. The mission of the enlightened is to pass on truth to others. Like a stone thrown into a pond, the effects ripple outward and have a far reaching impact. Furthermore, just as every piece in a gigantic puzzle is essential for the total view, each and every person is important. We all just need to use the opportunities we have been given to serve the larger purpose well and not waste those opportunities on foolish, childish things.

We have considered many of the ways religions have caused physical difficulties for people in handling their resources, emotions, future plans, priorities, morals and relationships throughout the ages. Let's look at how religions have complicated the intellectual or mental aspects of our lives. First of all, one's religious faith is intended to supersede all the rest of life's intellectual pursuits. Just as accepting the story of Santa Claus requires a child to reject all other reasonable perspectives of the way the world operates, so religions want their followers to yield their intellects to the other-world theologies they are taught. Worship starts with mental manipulation of what has happened in the past... and then it moves on to how the mind can be controlled to accept any counter intuitive event which conforms to the religious view of the world. In simple terms, idealistically, every religion requires the total subservience of the intellect. If the leaders hold fundamental power to make decisions in the religious tradition, they have the final word as to what the faithful should think. Essentially and ideally, one's religious faith is supposed to be the standard for all other life decisions. One is held captive so that all daily practical and political decisions are clarified within the religious tradition, no matter who might say otherwise. When one relies on one's faith for a long period of time, it's pretty difficult for any person to change or think differently.

What religions have decreed has been often accepted as intellectual truth, as wild, ridiculous or funny as that proposition or event in the past has appeared from outside the religion. Do believers change their minds when outsiders question their beliefs or ridiculous theology? Usually very few are intellectually moved to a new outlook. That's primarily because of the religion's long-standing tradition in history as well as in the beliefs of any one family. In fact, religious movements can get up in arms if their beliefs are too seriously challenged. For example, in as intellectually stimulated a country as the U.S., the subject of evolution can create quite a stir if the subject is called up for conversation. Such intellectual perspectives from around the world, multiplied by the great number of religions (say nothing about denominations) causes all kind of people to be leery about cooperation with or closeness to others even within the same community.

Religions requesting intellectual compliance also makes for significant difficulty in presenting a mature, real world analysis of truth. The time, concern, respectfulness, study and resources taken to keep everyone happy in a community is very demanding, especially in a world with so many vital concerns, calamities, conflicts and challenges. Where resources are in big demand, how can any government afford the wastefulness of silly diversions? Yet each group of religious zealots wants its fair share of attention, space, publicity and cooperation. How troubling this is to those who seriously want a chance to try to encourage a healthy intellectual climate in this chaotic world. The extensive differences between religious worldviews keeps almost everyone quiet and confused. Many of today's perspectives give almost everyone the idea that any philosophical or intellectual ideas are legitimate. This too makes it hard to get united, cooperative efforts for solutions to major earthly challenges. The human race is split up into a multitude of factions – all with competing elements and special axes to grind. How can such an atmosphere encourage a united approach to save the world, especially when a declining, deteriorating world gives some religions reason to assert that their god is in charge? When intellectual sharpness is critical for combating sloppy and diverse morality, little power and understanding is available to confused and dissimilar people. Look at immature people, fantasizing in their own little entertainment zones, reasonably comfortable and sheltered from the real world. They are people trying go escape the consequences of their egotistical activities and looking forward to imagined rewards down the road. People such as these – people caught up in such thinking – make it very difficult if not impossible to establish and coordinate harmonious, intellectual pursuits.

So the body and intellect is severely handicapped by fanciful tales about the realities of life, but we haven't yet touched what can occur within the human spirit. Many kinds of spiritual corruption infest the world when religions bring their irrational, confusing, unproven and even dirty laundry of creeds, principles, dogmas and standards to the table for analysis. When story telling is the popular game in town and the masses are held captive to the fast talkers, manipulators and people who tell lies for their own gain, there's not much that can be questioned or analyzed for real world understanding.

Most would agree that spiritual things are quite elusive even to insiders and leaders. Who stands out or makes the final decisions in any particular religion can boil down to who has the most friends in high places. Followers are usually not privy to what happens behind closed doors.

Spiritual corruption arises across the globe from many different religious perspectives – such serious impairment does not lag far behind spiritual visions and imaginary insights. Think about the scams that have taken place over the centuries where individuals have claimed special powers, insights or visions. What real world authority has been able to honestly call into question such events? Reports are made to excite and draw in the multitudes, but honest, straightforward evaluation is extremely rare. What does this kind of sensationalism do to or for the human spirit? Obviously, it degrades what the human spirit honestly has to offer. Moreover, it detracts from the real, credible accounts of human courage, vision and creativity in daily living. Even the publicity from such events or revelations pulls in a certain number of curios people susceptible to sensationalism. Clear thinking for healthy communities is hampered.

Because of religious distractions, the human spirit may be relegated to the short end of its potential in human development. The spirit of a person can be associated with courage, heart, emotion, essence, cheerfulness, mood, humor, personality, devotion and many other admirable qualities. If and when religions turn such qualities into primarily other-worldly attributes, the wonderful human spirit is lowered into second class status. When positive human attributes are put down for whatever reason, questions need to be raised as to how such a perspective relates to the real world in which we live. Human beings have made serious and consequential mistakes, but they also have been able to rise above their inadequacies for awesome accomplishments. In summary, the human body, mind and spirit are all in some peril when religious organizations spread their out of this world influence. Here's the flip side: The importance of telling the truth about our world is crucial for the mature development of the whole person. The truth frees human beings to grow up and focus on our present home and family.

The Story

The Santa Claus story gets started when parents want their child or children to get more entertained with Christmas. Of course, the Christmas celebration has changed over many centuries, but it's rooted in the birth of Jesus Christ. For the followers of Jesus, this was meant to be a Christian celebration. The giving of gifts was connected to the story of the gifts given to Jesus by the three wise men. As time went on, gift giving grew to where it is today – a very big, elaborate shopping spree that significantly stimulates the U.S. economy. For a long time, parents have wanted their children to enjoy this special season and consequently the gifts they receive have been connected to the gifts Jesus received. Santa Claus also has a long tradition of giving gifts at Christmas time, so it was natural that he too was incorporated into the gift giving. As the story grows, the all-knowing Santa could determine whether a child should or should not receive the desired gifts, according to the goodness or badness of the child's behavior. How convenient it was and is for parents to remind children of Santa when they needed a little more behavior control before Christmas. Not only that, but the whole fanciful story fits with the knowledge that people get rewarded these days for working hard, saying or doing the right things and being kind to others. Such a living standard works out good, even when there isn't a Santa.

So what happens when people are bad? They are punished. And who wants to reward children for being bad? We might not want to punish our children too severely for being bad, but at least they should not be rewarded. Consequently, the Santa story is useful to get people to conform and if they don't then there's hell to pay. But what happens when they learn the truth – that there is no Santa? True, some of the entertainment value is gone, but honestly we all know that whether we are good or bad the gifts will be delivered to most of us on Christmas Eve or Christmas morning. For parents' credibility sake, however, it would be best not to let the story continue too long. There might be other topics of discussion or moral codes that might be called into question if parents are not believable. The bottom line is that when struggling with life in the real world, entertaining stories will not give us any help in working out how we can survive day by day.

The Santa story is bogus. It might provide some entertainment for a while, but it's no good even for getting some leverage with behavior. Children need a lot of good direction even at an early age, and it's wise not to confuse them for long with an unreal world. Most people are in agreement that it's good if children are raised to get along, cooperate, understand, protect, clean up, learn, be proactive, and have good self-esteem. They don't need belief in Santa Claus to be motivated to do the right thing. Receiving too much from Santa (or anyone else) is also bad policy in a world of shortages. Where some children on our planet die of starvation and/or malnutrition, no one, not even children should receive too much. Enough is enough! There is enough for everyone around the world, but priorities need to be straightened out. Christmas excesses are bad for this whole planet that has finite resources. The fanciful stories used to extend or even continue such excesses are downright sad for the rich as well as the poor.

Adults as well as children have been told stories, maybe not for pure entertainment value, but certainly for leverage, power, conformity and material gain. How in the world did all these religious stories get started, and how in the world have these stories continued to flourish over the centuries? Maybe not too unlike the Santa stories, religions have entered a conflicted world in large part to fill a void. From the days before Christianity, the masses have been desperate for security in the present and for the future. The gods of the Egyptians and the Romans developed as a result of curiosity, concerns, moral ambiguity and maybe the biggest – insecurity. Stories and traditions grew... and people were swept up by the dreamed up fantasy ideas passed on by those who people thought were the experts and most knowledgeable of their contemporaries. What was believable? Any story that served someone's purpose and that made its way into the hearts and minds of large groups of despairing individuals, communities and nations. Coming into the time period of Jesus' life, the society and culture gave up on him because he wouldn't promise them what they wanted in benefits and security. As popular, wise, caring, loving, convincing and liberating as he was, he was killed on a cross because he wouldn't deliver what they wanted. The Christian religion was developed and expanded through decades of stories passed on from one person to another about their master – the chosen one. He fit the bill of one who had the power and authority to give people all they wanted, that is, if they could get it. That's where his so called followers or disciples fit in. They embellished the story and simply added what the people couldn't get from Jesus while he was alive. So the stories grew... as they were passed along from one to another... and as they were put into rudimentary handwriting... and finally, as they were creatively translated and put into print... and we must add, with leaders (who had all kinds of axes to grind) laying out the detailed accounts. What an extended, fanciful process was used to advance the natural inclination for material security and endless life. Could there be any reservations about the truth of the story? You know the answer.

Things didn't change much over the centuries. If anything the narratives just got bigger and harder to understand. However, the tradition deepened and the religious authorities continued to reinforce their power over the followers. What was the alternative to attaining eternal life? No cost of requirements and conditions seemed to be too much. So what had been told throughout the ages became established almost as a kind of recital of the truth for daily living. Little, if anything, was questioned and most thinking people conformed without much fuss. The story became the accepted testimony of human development. Other cultures and races which had been left out turned to their own versions of the story – their own religions – seemingly also committed to giving their constituencies everything they wanted. A wonderful life after death (or eternal life as the story goes) was the prize. Religions and the leaders of such movements had people and their resources in the palms of their hands. Has anything changed over the past 2,000 years? We have had to recognize that a very large percentage of the world's population is still feeling very insecure and the account of dreamy after-life is very attractive.

What's the story today? Religious doctrines are accepted as the truths above all others by a very large share of the world's present population, even though these doctrines have almost no factual credibility. Almost no one wants to take on the powerful religious establishment, no matter what the cost might be to the world's continuing existence. Seemingly, the most important consideration for a good present and future life is one's personal salvation. Let the world take care of itself, or better yet, let god take care of it! That's the prevailing story around the world. Will humanity ever grow up and face our real world and do what should be done to care for our global brothers and sisters and the one and only home we will ever know?

Yes, religions have rushed in to fill the void of people finding lasting security, but there are other impulses which have inspired people to get attached to religions irrationally. Explanations for the creation of the world (which human beings have searched for throughout time) have been a part of the answers religions have provided to inquisitive people. Before the rise of science in our modern world, not many facts of life about the earth were available to the average person. The earth was said to be flat until relatively recent times. Poor information was better than no information for a population that was searching for answers to an unexplored globe. Still, even today in a world of vast educational resources, reasonably intelligent religious followers look at their religious resources as scientific facts. They block out other perspectives as wrong, unbelievable or threatening to their religious faith. Why? How can a realistic, competent, documented, insightful and helpful view of this earth be rejected? The story they have heard time and time again and that their parents and grandparents have believed for ages is deeply ingrained in their minds and personalities. Especially as creatures of habit, they continue their problematic thinking in the face of the basic facts of life. The story has been repeated, ingrained and personalized too long. In essence, religion has turned them into little more than robots that spew out what has been funneled into them. The world could be destroyed before they would see the light. Here again religion has had a disastrous impact on our very special planet. How tragic, since this is our only infinitely small globe – one positioned properly in a mysterious universe. This is the beautiful, delicate, valuable world in which we live.

Another cause for concern about religious doctrine is that it usually aligns the referenced, tangible, material world against what is put together concerning the intangible, fantasy world. Which side should a person take if one's eternal life is on the line or at minimum the focus of attention? It doesn't take a wizard to figure that one out. So naturally, believing religious dogma is exceedingly important to religious leaders. It determines their success, power and material blessings. Not only do these leaders compete with other religious leaders but they also compete with all that is experienced tangibly by people in their everyday lives. As powerful and influential as religions can be, this competition can make for real struggles. Some of this is happening in the U.S. today as materialism grows more rampant and religious participation seems to be declining. What can be done other than to complain about how gross materialism and a me first mentality ruins everything good about this life... as well as risks one's chance for eternal life. This is the criticism that seems to affect wise people the most and backs them off from the criticism of religions in general.

It's probably not so surprising that so many people are swept away with religious testimony in our day and age. What's at the top of the news? It's often the awesome, popular sports figure, or the music sensation (or trend setter) that gives his or her witness. Check out the many notables on T-V or in movies or magazines that are getting carried away. This can be associated with the popular point to the sky testimony of the athlete who has made some awesome play and wants to (as they say) give god the glory. That certainly is part of the story's impact on contemporary living. Some look forward (literally) to the day they get carried away in a cloud. But let's get more to the point of emotionalism. Religions have captivated millions in order to get them to express their most heart-felt commitments to their leaders and any imagined ultimate authority. Religious leaders have been witnesses to the facts of their own conversion to the intangible and unseen. The religious testimony preached to anyone willing to hear has been shouted from the rooftops, so to speak. There has been nothing more inspired and emotionalized than the personalized accounts of preachers, prophets and evangelists. Naturally they all receive their benefits from enthusiastic proclamation. But the many little ones who have had nothing to lose have been very open and vulnerable to religious preaching, teaching, counseling and healing. Emotions play a very important role in otherworldly enthusiasm and commitment. Who doesn't like a story told with apparent conviction and dedication? Worship centers around the world showcase in many ways the attractiveness of lives given to divine stories of dedication and commitment. Questioners are won over to repeated stories of past saints who have been held high for others to emulate. Yes, the religious story repeated over and over has been very attractive indeed... as frivolous, abstract and absolute as it has been presented. It certainly does rival the child's Santa Claus story. The trouble is, it's for adults.

Changing

Moving from one way of looking at life to another way of thinking about it is usually not an easy process. Changing from seeing all of life in a religious way to seeing life without a strong religious input can alter thought patterns as well as well as daily activities. As human beings with a long history of coping with our surrounding world, we have been and still are creatures of habit. It has helped us to survive in a very competitive environment. When past guidance for decisions and activities was mapped out by strong religious ties and influential accommodating leadership, life seemed comfortable, predictable and pleasant. The people around us who had help to nurture us in our religious faith were helpful, gave us a constant sense of security and even gave us insights into what life might be like beyond the grave. All seemed right with the world. Then there comes a challenge to reject a major part of the picture – the part that really captivated our whole world view and beyond. In such a new way of thinking and living there would be... no god to pray to in order to get help in difficult times, no need for a reference to heaven or hell, no need to follow a specific moral code, no putting off for eternity what should be done today or tomorrow, no impressive, promised reward for the greatness of one's identity as a unique human being, no reason to try to win over non-believers, no religious doctrines or dogmas to memorize and apply to present circumstances and finally, no pressure to worship any special deity. While that brings a lot of nos into working out what life is all about, it also brings a lot of questions and insecurities into the equation. A person might begin to feel like a fish out of water – not a comfortable experience. After saying all that, it must be admitted there is a certain difficult, hard to handle truth to all the above comments about the changes we are contemplating.

What a radical change means to a human being is not without serious difficulties. That's why not many people can negotiate significant change. That's also why change is best handled over long periods of time. Think of the long term adjustments that the human race as well as individuals have made. For example, think about the issue concerning whether the world was flat or round, about a changing a form of transportation, a political revolution, or even losing a member of the family. Change can be hard, long and seemingly insurmountable. But it can and does take place with persistence and over a long period of time. Very few people are willing to go back to where they were after they have mastered important new vistas.

Changing one's religion or essentially dropping religion altogether has to be one of the most challenging things a faithful follower could ever accomplish. It's right up there with the all- encompassing problem of alcoholism. Any true alcoholic is completely controlled by his or her addiction. Alcoholism has become the person's whole life. To make a change often requires a crisis, a willingness to give up one's control of many things, some special help and a lot of willingness to negotiate the unknown. One could suspect, that for a small child, giving up the idea of Santa Claus is truly child's play. That's not the case with being willing as an adult to give up a significant number of one's religious beliefs and traditions to living out life in an acceptable manner. So, suggesting that some important religious pronouncements are lies to gain conformity and loyalty is a lot to swallow. This is maybe the place to say that one of the first suggestions about the flat world being round is usually not taken seriously, is thought to be crazy, is hard to present and is out-rightly rejected. However, if the suggested world view is indeed truth for the long term future, it can be regarded as a first step toward a kind of new world for future generations. If the suggested change is not worth promoting or is wrong for the future, the change will undoubtedly collapse in due time.

At this early stage of stating that the religious view of meriting eternal life is bad for the world, there certainly is more than one point of view. Still, there's no turning back from stating what many people will see as obvious when they have a chance to think about it. Who can argue against the real, critical, provable, historical and obvious situation we live in? Who can argue for life after death, which is totally an unknown? Change is necessary, but is it possible given the long history of religions? The religious responsibility for our present problem is so obvious it's almost laughable, if it weren't so sad and politically incorrect. It must be admitted off the top, few people would openly suggest that religions (which have honestly done a lot of good in the world) might be the cause of the world's conflict and deterioration. Yet the case can and should be made for change in the more extreme offerings religions have made to susceptible people. In essence, the promise of eternal life (as one of the most critical, earth shaking and dreamy dogmas for most religions) has been a downright disaster for individuals, faithful followers, non-believers and the present condition of the whole world. This is no inconsequential charge. Furthermore, this fantasy of the after-life will become (if it already isn't) a tipping point for the future of human life on earth.

Do we presently have enough of a world crisis to suggest some changes? You can bet on it, if you are a betting person. Exactly how long we have life as we know it on our planet is certainly very debatable. At our current place in history, we may not have the time (considering the slow pace of change) to alter our course of deteriorating political, economic, cultural and environmental conditions. How long would it take to being the world back to real health and happiness? How long would it take for the human race to face up to its responsibilities and try to correct some serious flaws in many aspects of our lives? How long would it take, starting this very instant, for us to harmonize our various economies, cultures and traditions so that we could start working together for some serious solutions? Your guess is probably as good as mine.

Yes, changing will take some time. It always does. Still, change is also inevitable. We in the U.S. will not be the same people in a decade that we are today. The only question is what direction will we go and what will be the consequences? I believe the human spirit argues for life that is sustainable, healthy, prosperous, economical, good for all of created life on earth and intelligent to the best of human ability. Human beings have the potential to do so much better than what we have done, but we have been carried away by egotistical, powerful and greedy people that have ruined things for the whole creation. How can goodness overcome badness without depending on using irrational, fanciful leverage that pulls ignorant innocents down into terrifying and terrible decisions which in the end will bring us all to a bad and sad ending?

The question about change is meant to be concrete and not a frivolous question. What can we as individuals do about change in our own lives? The answer to that question is simple – as simple as a personal decision now, even in the midst of reading this book. We must remember that good change takes place very slowly, and if that change moves a person in even a simple creative, up-building and healthy way, it will be good for the whole world. We must remember the importance of the one piece of the puzzle. There is no simple, rational, scientific, one size fits all formula for what should be done because there are endless things that should and can be done to come back to health and happiness. The one necessary element is that there must be change – healthy, creative, beneficial change. Not to change is to give up, deteriorate and die. The dinosaurs could not change enough in their limited abilities... and also considering their critical circumstances. It would be truly tragic if human beings with their vast abilities and opportunities could not change their circumstances enough to eliminate slow extinction... all the while looking forward to some fantasy life after death. This would probably be the most ultimate tragedy for the entire universe. To state the obvious, change is necessary, but it does bring along conflicts.

Conflicts

Thinking about children and the story they've been told about Santa Claus, we would do well to consider that there are both good and bad features to this story. Let's start out with the bad. Since children have so much faith in their parents at a young age, there is no question that when the truth is finally acknowledged that there is no Santa Claus, there's a certain loss of faith in the story teller. That's especially true when the story is carried forward a long period of time. A second bad issue concerns the loss of leverage when there is no Santa Claus watching the child's every move. The naughty and nice business has to be let go, even though parents can remind children that if they don't obey or behave, they themselves can hold back on the presents. Another possible loss for both parents and children is changing the traditions, images and fantasy associated with Santa's coming. Often, some of the family fun and games associated with Christmas fall to the wayside.

Of course there is a good side to telling the truth. Children grow up fast and they learn a lot of truth from every facet of their environment – whether from their friends, teachers, associates, sources of news or just from the world in which they live. The truth has a way of leaking through in almost every moment of our lives, whether we are children or adults. Of course, there is less pampering as children grow more responsible, inquisitive and knowledgeable. That means that they are entering a less fanciful world and one more concrete. Children need the straight facts in order to learn how to survive and of course parents desperately want this for their offspring. Another bonus is that more honest conversations can take place when the story telling stops. But there are still more advantages to coming clean early in a child's life. Both parents and children can get away from hiding things and being deceptive. When a child begins to think about honest gift-giving rather than about what he or she is going to get from Santa, there can be a new sense of gift-giving and caring about others. Then there can be a lot more beneficial conversations with the whole world outside the child's immediate surroundings. A benefit not often considered is what living with the truth means to a person's self-image. What does concern about one's knowledge of truth and falsehood do to affect the daily tasks of growing up? What happens when inner belief comes into conflict with outside realities? And finally, simply a realistic, honest, liberating view of the world means not only a better chance for survival but also a much more responsible outlook for all immediate, personal decisions.

Now, by this time, we as adults can't help but start thinking about how the above two paragraphs relate to our relationship to religions and all that those ancient traditions ask us to believe. Again, let's begin with what would be lost without them. Really, that's a rather complex issue. There is no question that the religions of the world have been deeply involved with the arts and endless creative endeavors throughout the ages. What kind of world would we experience today without these magnificent, flourishing, creative and expressive contributions by countless people? Religious buildings have reflected awesome inspiration, life-long labor, beautiful designs and fanciful imagination. In addition, religious leaders have been an integral part of good community life almost everywhere. What would life on our planet be without them? Finally, how could religious messages be changed to reflect the real world we live in today? Trying to answer these kinds of questions is what some people would call tough sledding. How does passing on a new, honest perspective on life help people adjust to life without religion? This would be an endless, challenging and dangerous task. And how can the religious story be straightened out to convey the difference between truth and fiction? Word of mouth does not let human beings easily ascertain the truth about life long ago.

As religions have provided humanity with a lot of good insights to study and absorb over long periods of time and so have controlled a significant place even in contemporary thought and action, so also religions have impacted human history in almost unbelievable, tragic and seductive ways. There could be a lot learned from a realistic assessment of what religions have offered, required and inspired throughout history. We have noted things religions have offered the world which would be missed. But we also know there is another side. Sad to say there is a lot to consider. Reading the news today about a mass killing of 50 people in Florida, we find out that the killer (who was himself killed) was a religious person and had strong feelings about certain issues. We need not go any further than this in our analysis of that situation to realize that every religion has followers with strong feelings about certain issues. Has there been any movement in human history which has divided people up, moved them to extremes, caused them to put down others and even inspired them to defeat and destroy unbelievers more than religions? This factor in itself would be a good enough reason to assert that religions have done more to hurt humanity than to help it. Think about the conflict (from personal to international) that has been caused basically by religious perspectives over the centuries. Hatred, wars and mass killings are just a few of the terrible consequences of people being caught up in their religious beliefs. If religions were to quit promoting their fantasies and retract their fabricated doctrines, what a difference that would make to encourage what religions have done right. But let's move on to some other realities when religious ideologies are in control.

Every religion has its big stories to tell. Those stories expressed usually by word of mouth are what excite and inspire people. The better or more elaborate, captivating or beneficial the story, the more enthusiastic the converts. Time usually just enhances the details and the dreams for non-objective, innocent, ignorant and wishful people. And so the story goes and grows – generation after generation. Who would be daring enough to take issue with the tall tales and downright lies told for ulterior motives? We would be wise to acknowledge that there have been many people connected to many religions who have used their so called religious inspiration to pad their power and/or their pocketbooks. Every once in a while, a person might be caught in a lie or exaggeration and exposed for fraud. But those occurrences are rare when religion is involved.

Here is a big question. Have there been instances where religious leaders have used their power or religious authority to take advantage of those under their care? The comeback to that question is, "Are you kidding?"

In an era when news travels like wildfire, the Christian Church has been nearly gutted by such instances. What has been the comeback other than to try to cover up the sad, sick and terrible occurrences? What could the god of such a religion think about such leadership and authority figures? Of course, discussions about what goes on behind closed doors are muted or silenced around those who want to believe. The beautiful, influential, caring, Christian Church should be kept looking as pretty as possible, shouldn't it? I would guess that the Christian religion is not the only religion with skeletons in the closet.

Where does the Christian religion stand with regard to real life in this 21st century? Where does it stand with regard to the best and most honest human insights of our modern era? What does it say about science along with the facts of the universe we are beginning to peek into today? The answer to those questions is pretty much silence. A good chunk of Christianity puts the Bible ahead of science as a truth teller about creation. A good chunk of the religion rejects the science about climate change and human influence. This can be said within the boundaries of the most advanced technological society ever on the face of the globe. Pretty much the rest of the religious establishment in the U.S. is silent about how the Bible interacts with science. Apparently, there would be too much answering to do to too many of its members. How's that for honesty and telling the truth and following "The Way, The Truth and The Life?" It's sad to have to explain to believing church members that the Bible was never written as a book of science but simply as a book of faith. It's also sad to say that it could very well be that a good share of the Bible was put together as a gathering of tall tales around some very important nuggets of historical truth. When will the leadership of the Christian religion realize that it should come clean for the sake of the world and not continue to baby its membership with fantasy stories? When will the religious authorities face the facts and admit there is no Santa Claus?

An important and possibly critical element concerning the impact religions have had... has to do with how resources have been used. Waste is hardly an adequate word. Followers have contributed whatever to please their gods and secure their rewards. Think about the amount of time, work, money, talents and heart that the faithful have paid, given or donated throughout their lives. What for? To please their gods? What for? To get to heaven? Have all these resources enhanced the basic tenets of world religions or have they been diverted to salaries, buildings, trinkets, advertising and pontificating? Consider how these nearly endless resources could have been used to truly do the will of a creator (if there is one) and make this world and all its living forms more healthy, happy, secure and worthwhile. In an era of realizing there are limited world assets (where people go hungry, are without shelter and medical care, feel neglected and abused, etc.), priorities are critical for a healthy, happy planet. Much has been destroyed or used irresponsibly. So what will be done with what we still have for the real world and its critical needs? The perspective the human race will have on religion and life in a fantasy world may help decide whether the world lives in renewal or dies a slow death.

Religions have not provided people with good self-images or the inspiration to get along with foreigners. They generally have focused on storytelling to get leverage (control) for payment and loyalty; and then they have glamorized the afterlife to cater to personal fear and insecurity. While such tools may work with small children, neither of these have been helpful or useful for mature individuals. Having one's thinking controlled with fantasies does not make for a life of freedom to grow and develop, even though it may get some payback. Furthermore, a person needs to feel good about themselves in order to be able to contribute adequately. The world desperately needs its human population to grow up and act maturely and responsibly. The world has gone too long with a fanciful species that has tended to overlook what it has done detrimentally in the past. Also, glamorizing the after-life has enabled people to escape the real world and focus on their own personal salvation... letting the rest of the world go to hell. That too has enabled individuals to be irresponsible in their relationships with people unlike themselves. There is no way that our world can survive without a cooperative relationship among all its inhabitants. Trying to escape personally into another life can't benefit the earth's family now, say nothing about how pointless the efforts are to try to make sure one will have another life. Religions today need to help all people forget their fantasies, grow up, and take responsibility for the life they have been given. Those who have been religious in the past need to learn to use their lives to enhance the world around them, practice living in peace with toleration for differences with others, and finally, enjoy their moments on earth, letting future life or living move into mystery.

There is no question that religions have made some positive contributions to the world even since the beginning of recorded time. However, those contributions do not outweigh the detrimental impact that they have made in history. Just as the story of Santa is innocent in the beginning and provides some fun and games, religion has provided some of the same kind of dreamy diversion from hard realities. In the end, however, a good measure of religious requirements and promises are disastrous for the integrity of the world and lead us into a horrible way to live on earth responsibly. It is true that it will take some time for human beings to separate what has been a disaster in religious doctrine from what has been based on reality and what has been helpful in the development of human history. But it can and should be done, no matter how much time it takes. Every step back from a life of fantasy can be a step forward in liberation and mature, insightful, co-operative and healthy living. Little by little in each individual's small contributions and insights, a lot can become evident among many contributors. Evidence can become overwhelmingly clear in the transformation of turning around what the world has been to what the world can become. That kind of faith is grounded in reality.

To Save the World

Save the world – could there be a more outlandish suggestion for an earth-shaking essay than the proposal of these three words? Could there be a more crucial issue for the human race, if indeed the world is deteriorating or dying? Do the people on this planet have the power to bring the world back from the brink of disintegration and death? These are questions that may come to mind as we struggle to stay afloat as individuals, families, communities and nations, early in the 21st century. No project may be bigger or more important than this one. The world is our life and living. The world is our home.

Does the world need saving? Some people might not think so. Of course there are always two sides of any argument. But if we want to act grown up, let's look at the facts. In many ways religions have corrupted and deteriorated the world. To move away from the bad influence they have had over the centuries, followers will need to be led to this truth in a careful, straightforward and honest manner. There needs to be patience in this transformation along with a careful analysis of exactly where religions have gone wrong. It won't be an easy sell, since the stories and experiences are extensive, have been repeated generation after generation and have emotional roots among the masses. But the key to this transformation is in focusing on the new, very important reality of becoming mature and responsible human beings. We need to carry forward the important agenda of saving our home and family. Unlike simply being wrapped up with following orders and striving for self-preservation in connection with going to heaven after death (which individuals have almost no control over), this exciting and challenging mission can affect all of life in the real world. Such a mission rewards concrete actions benefiting our global home and international family. This is a massive new look at our world. A new approach should be taken with people who need to learn how to cooperate with one-another and live in peace. There is the added challenge of figuring out how to, putting it simply, save the world. That's something that the human race can and should do in the future. We have the capability if we set our minds to the task at hand. There can be no "visions of sugarplums" to sugar coat our present problems or deflect what must be done as soon as possible.

Let's look at a number of aspects of this gigantic, political (the work of the people) change. Simply, trying to learn to live in the present (rather than to live in dreamland or in the future) will be difficult for many religious people. The concrete world in which we live is hard to understand and handle on a daily basis. People are not perfect and we often want to try to escape the hard reality of dealing with them. That's obviously why many try to escape into religious fantasies, say nothing of into drugs or even into sacrificing their lives. Imagine the hard work of helping nearly hopeless individuals work through daily difficulties without depending upon escapes. Working in the present can be exciting and rewarding if one considers the benefits that can be felt by individual pieces of our planet moving to a better and more healthy place. Even in the face of death, whether in a healthy or desperate individual, inhabitants of our world can be helped to understand that out of death can come new life. It happens every day in every spot on the globe. In facing and living in the present, every tiny piece of the puzzle has its important place in the universe. In reality, there is no getting around it. What is beyond this truth is mystery, which itself is absolutely wonderful. The only thing lost in this newness is our focus on the ego and a fantasy life beyond the world.

One key requirement for a world without religions is establishing a moral code acceptable to most if not all the nations of the world. Of course that moral code could be gleaned from one or more religions of the world or put together by specialists representing as many people as possible. Such a code could start out as fundamentals for basic human behaviors and developed over time as the need arises. One important consideration is how and where good moral codes have functioned well for almost all people in the past. A good example of starting new is the development of the constitution of the United States. On the other hand, over 2,000 years of history can point to successes as well as failures in how people can function together with cooperation and peace. History is a good teacher, but modern science and various national political experiments could also provide excellent guiding principles for going through the process of establishing a moral code appropriate for moving toward the goal of saving the world. Poor moral codes in the past have been a large part of the problem of a world in decline and threatened by extinction. Consequently, going forward, the world's inhabitants need to establish a good, practical, insightful moral code in order to accomplish basic survival. Impressing this reality on everyone will be difficult but totally necessary when we have a larger view of our planet. How fast the human race can begin to set in motion steps toward a common vision of good and acceptable world government will be critically important to whether our species lives far into the future or dies likes the dinosaurs. Can we find a good, solid, refreshing, healthy, healing, human morality in time for healthy, happy living? Growing up needs to happen fast!

Getting down to the basics for a thriving world's population will require digging into the whole question of what it means to be fully human. Various religions have attempted to get at this question of utmost importance. What place do we have in the universe? Outside of fantasies, what purpose do we serve as citizens of our planet? Can we accept a limited role as humans amid the almost limitless forms of life around us? What will it mean to grow up into a responsible species capable of affecting the vigorous development or tragic destruction of our only realized home? Can people in this 21st century find it in them to change the course of history from living immaturely to living responsibly? Understanding what it means to be fully human will necessitate the realization that we do not resemble god, that god is of our own making, that any ultimate force does not have a special place for each of us to dwell in the future, that we are all important in today's reality as we care for ourselves and our world, that each person can and does make a difference in the eternal scheme of things and that what we do or don't do today will determine the future of our planet. That's the reality of life as we know it today. We have been richly blessed and we have the potential in our humanity to richly bless others – today and forever. It simply takes new, creative actions. This is our spectacular, creative freedom to enjoy day by day.

In order to save the world it will be critical that all people learn how to communicate well with one another. In our present age, technology has enabled us to pass messages to one another around the world at an awesome pace. Still, that has not enabled us to understand or feel for those unlike ourselves. There are too many barriers, set up by too many egos, enabled by too many fantasies. Yet good communication could take place, if our lives depended on it. And our lives do depend upon it. In order to save the world, each of us needs to begin to feel what a different person feels and not get lost in self-centered behavior. Big egos and self-centered behavior simply built up barriers which have destroyed communication, cooperation and caring. Caring about how others feel can enable new visions, new opportunities, new possibilities and even new life to sprout up. Trying to find places of sharing, accommodating and yielding will usually bring out the best in anyone on the opposite side of the table. Sadly, what we are doing today is just the opposite of what should be done for the world's survival. We have been in the competition mode instead of in the self-giving mode. A competitive attitude assures defeats where an expression of self-giving encourages sharing. That fact should be obvious, but it isn't too immature, egocentric individuals. Consequently, we witness the roots and history of destruction. Communication is not done just with words or sign language but also and most clearly with good deeds done to pass on benefits. From here a multiplication process begins to build a better home and a more caring family. Honestly, more deeply felt up-building communication among inhabitants can accelerate the refreshment of the earth. Vast, new opportunities lie ahead of us in the real world.

Improving communication can and will increase harmony among many races, cultures and nations. But harmony is needed not only between members of the same species but also between all forms of life. This may well be a relatively new area of challenge for humans. Not respecting or valuing many forms of life in the past has caused even our own species certain difficulties. Living things on our planet have been woven together very creatively over thousands if not millions of years, and when even one small part of life on earth is lost or destroyed, pressure and difficulty is applied to many other forms of life. We are beginning to understand how intertwined we all are as inhabitants of our planet. We need to function together with deep sensitivity concerning what is essential or basically needed for extending quality living for all our various partners. Yes, needing to look at how to save the world might very well be even a bigger challenge for us than how to travel far out into space. It takes an orchestra a very long time to merge many and varied instruments into creating and perfecting a beautiful, harmonious piece of music. Yet the fundamental harmony of blending together all forms of life on earth for healthy, creative meaningful life will require the very best human beings have to offer forever. How can we even begin to think about how to blend religions, nations and races with all other living things to highlight the growing potential of the earth? It's time we gave up the game playing and got started... one key stroke at a time.

Going about "the earth saving business" in ways we human beings can manage at this point in time also requires us to utilize the very best resources we can dig out of the past. For hundred and even thousands of years humanity has accomplished some good things, even as the world has radically changed. Nations, religions, cultures and races have made imprints on our human history that are amazing even to modern men and women. People from every spot on the globe should be able to take pride in what has been accomplished and find the inspiration to build on those cornerstones laid down by our ancestors. Looking back, we can learn that often simple people accepted rather incomprehensible proposals in order to move forward in their concrete lives and accomplish their specific often limited goals. Today we should be able to learn from their courage and determination that we too can adapt to new ways of handling the rigors of life. Our advantage is that we can see and contemplate what has been done in the past. That should enable us to understand we can now begin to go about the larger tasks ahead of us with some measure of confidence.

There is a lot of correcting that needs to be clarified

and implemented by knowledgeable people. Generally, the best scientific leaders would be those people who can truly understand how change can and should take place. It doesn't take even the average person long to figure out some of the imbalances we now have in our world and the losses we have sustained. Our world has evolved and will continue to do so. There's no such thing as the perfect world, so we should not hesitate to try our best to do what we can do, in the time we have in front of us. The best changes take place over extended periods of time anyway. What might be the hardest challenge to handle is attempting to correct the important losses we feel and have experienced in the recent past. In some cases, we may be able to resurrect what has been eliminated and has been at a significant cost to life in general. Other forms of life we may have destroyed may have to be let go, even as a trauma center in a hospital needs to admit certain losses and move on to other critical cases. In order to save the world, the process of growing up for modern men and women will be a real struggle to find responsible decision making. But what's the alternative to pursuing maturity and doing one's best? Certainly we dare not be living in a deteriorating dreamland looking toward certain death down the road.

Our environment certainly is critical for sustaining life. There's nothing more important to figure out and get on life support, since we already are feeling the effects of deterioration and impending chaos. Melting ice caps, rising oceans, radical weather patterns, loss of life-giving forests, droughts, fires, exploding populations, loss of atmosphere protection, the growing separation between the rich and the poor, terrorism from people willing to die in order to kill, an outrageous, billionaire politician (running for President of the United States) yelling for more fire arms and for closing more doors, religious people supporting the more for me mentality – these are some of the crisis points facing today's world. All this rolls together as part of the environment we live in. Most of the major environmental crises are a result of human greed, mismanagement and corruption. Finally, should this critical, environmental disaster be put on life support? Or is this a case too far gone? Of course we can't give up on the world's depressing condition, because it's absolutely critical for all forms of life. How long can humanity let our present deteriorated state continue to get worse? Will dreamland or maybe prayers intervene in this advancing world-wide hurricane? Let's get serious. Our environment is the whole package surrounding each and every one of us. It's not only we human beings beginning to suffer the environmental degradation but also all the other innocent creatures of the world.

Getting into the real challenges of making the world a better place in which to live, there is one very important commodity which would make an awesome difference for the world's survival. That commodity is sacrifice. We know that human beings have been willing to sacrifice even their lives for religious ideals, family protection, their country and other such things. Most of us applaud such examples of offering everything for a great purpose. Considering what has been done, it's certainly within reach for a better informed world to attempt to inspire maturing human beings to see the wonderful value of sacrificing even a little for the life of the world – for humans and all other forms of life. The kinds of sacrifice that would be very important are the kinds that would reduce our human egos, be willing to cut back luxurious consumption, let go of religious fantasies, seriously diminish intolerance and delete resistance to change. Yes, sacrifice for others, giving up advantages for the sake benefiting our home and family, yielding power to increase cooperation and harmony, these kinds of efforts should be part of the new initiatives for people to welcome and celebrate for life-saving. Considering what has been happening throughout the world – that competition, threats, greed and power have been mostly in play – the change in the vision of a new way of living would not be easy. Still, it has also been a slow, agonizing process getting into such a deteriorated condition. We need to understand that the goal of living for life-giving enhancements cannot be given up, even if we work for that goal only to make things better for our own children and grandchildren. Religions have stressed sacrifice as an action worth pursuing in this real world of limitations and vulnerabilities. So it's not unthinkable to suggest the appropriateness of moving forward with sacrificial actions to be a part of the re-creation process. Not only does present life on earth merit our best efforts (after such a long time drifting in the opposite direction) but future generations will especially be affected by whatever we do or don't do. Here is where the rubber hits the road. We will be held accountable by the state of the universe for either trying to save the world or for neglecting it and letting it die. We stand a crucial crossroads. Really, the only question is whether we have the will to act sacrificially... as well as have the time to turn things around.

It is uplifting to realize and say again that good, solid, creative, enduring change doesn't happen overnight but makes its presence known over a long period of time. That fact can free a person to simply think and act maturely and appropriately in the reality of the present moment. Being set free from concerns about which we have no influence, we can be uplifted to simply do our best in the present and future for our home and family. There will be great honor in this endeavor. Helping stressed, depressed and deteriorating victims move out of critical care into a place of healing and future health is no small task. It has been praised in the past and it will be even more valued in the future. The urgency is to hang in there, continue be to try to do better, solidify the vision of a renewing world and be willing to wait and look for life-giving results for present and future generations. The world has not evolved overnight and it will continue to evolve forever. The real mind blowing opportunity is that our species can desire to be affecting positive change and new life spurred on in this very moment.

Learning to nurture all of life's forms for the sake of all living things will take a lot of openness and determined inquiry. How can we interact with wisdom, dedication and sacrifice for the good of the whole world? One thing we must realize early on is that every part of the earth's creation must accept its limits and so must yield respectfully and responsibly to benefit the whole. Now for human beings, that realization is quite a switch. From long ago, we were told our faith begins with fantasizing that each person will live in heaven, with desires met, surrounded by angels, preserved with the creator god forever. So what should we think today? What should people who have been born on this planet believe in an age of science and advanced technology? We know now that life should be treasured and nurtured. It is also very vulnerable to deterioration, decline and death. With these facts, it's incumbent upon us to use every benefit we have been given to make good use of our time for a proper purpose. Learning to nurture and benefit what the world provides will certainly be advantageous in many ways. Caring for life around us will be continuing to do what has been done creatively in moving us along from the world's beginnings. The sad realization is that our species could kill the whole process. In fact, humanity is presently moving the whole planet in that direction. There's a big difference between nurturing and destroying... and human beings hold the key to what will happen in the future. Will we have the time to grow up?

There is something that could be very helpful in our search for truth and reality. It could also clear away a lot of religion's fantasies. Science is the truth teller before us today, but sad to say it has not been readily accepted by enough people and politicians. One of the primary reasons for this is that science cannot play along with much of religious doctrine. That puts science at odds with most immature people who want to believe the stories they have been told in order to assure themselves of the prize of eternal life. Many of the religious faithful have chosen to go along with the traditional fanciful stories they have heard or read rather than face reality. They are mentally and emotionally tied to a long tradition of fabrications meant to control them and give them the security they so desperately seek. These people normally have been in a weak position intellectually and emotionally and seemingly have had to go along with religious authorities almost as a matter of survival. How can science candidly oppose the emotions and fantasies of the vast, overpowering religious world? Science has not forsaken the truth, but neither has it stated clearly what's at stake for getting humanity to face the world's disturbing condition. It must be said that science needs to assert itself and speak up candidly and forcefully for the sake of the world's life. It's not that science has all the answers since much of the truth and factual evidence for human beings is still hidden or continuing to be mystery. But with more encouragement, scientific knowledge can advance our understanding of this troubling world around us and potentially lead us into a much greater maturity about what needs to be done for the long term survival and refreshment of our planet. It is imperative for us to open up our minds and hearts to those who have rigorously studied the world. We need to listen to the voices of reason, intellectual authenticity, and scholarly advice to counter what we have so emotionally absorbed in the past without question or verification.

The human spirit cannot be denied, contained or destroyed on this complex and troubling planet. The human spirit has overcome immense barriers and confrontations over the centuries relative to life and death issues, national conflicts, physical deprivations, racial prejudices and global crises. Nothing has been too large or complex for this earth's inhabitants to face and manage. Even though our spirit has never really contemplated our responsibility for the world's condition, there is no reason to think that a coordinated, cooperative and wise proposition to save our home and family couldn't be established. Not all people need to be on board for a successful transition toward recreating a healthy planet, but the resilient and creative spirit of even a few leaders could lead the rest of the world forward into a more healthy and happy situation. The human spirit does not need religion and its tall tales to be alive and well. When we think back to history's great personalities, we can begin to contemplate the great and wonderful things that can be done, truth be told. What has held back individuals who have accepted a vision of something vastly better than what was being experienced? Nothing. No doubts, threats, complexities, barriers or even uncontrollable events have been able to extinguish what a person with an inspired vision has to offer. Certainly thinking people out of their very souls will be able to make exciting and valuable contributions for the welfare of all. The human spirit is alive and well today, even though it may be terribly misinformed or misdirected. If the world is to be saved as time goes on, we can be certain that the creative spirits of men and women will be in the forefront of leading us away from deterioration and disaster with hopefulness. They will undoubtedly see themselves as simply small pieces of an awesome, wondrous, beautiful picture or vision. Every spirit is a piece and has a place. Yes, each and every human being can make a contribution to this special place in the universe. Only mystery moves beyond our home and family. We are not responsible for that. We just take what we get. We accept mystery and wait for it to be revealed.

What is our attitude as we begin to peek into our mission of saving the world? We cannot be arrogant about taking part in such a mission since we have been a real part of the problem. A child being told the truth (if the truth is being accepted) does not feel especially wise, proud or satisfied with the new revelation. The feeling may be more related to embarrassment, shame or feeling foolish. Actually, that initial response is not all that bad for wisely and emotionally handling future responsibilities. In a sense, we all feel a bit drained when we hear a sad but convincing presentation about our past immaturity. We are humbled. Interestingly enough, that happens to be the ideal time to begin the rebuilding process. Openness to new, factual, instructive and challenging information which inspires freedom and opportunity can be exceedingly beneficial in the process of growing up. So it is that witnessing a sense of humility and thankfulness for finally getting the truth is heartwarming as well as exciting to those responsible for getting across the difficult new reality or a vision of the truth. In fact, both teachers and students can inspire one another in giving and accepting information. In the process of sharing, the personal qualities of humility and thankfulness are nearly impossible for a witness to ignore or toss aside. Essentially these two qualities are infectious, contribute to benevolence and often inspire imitation. What the world desperately wants and needs in a time of crisis are a few caring, humble and thankful spirits. A handful of those hopeful individuals can inspire and refresh our world's most desperate condition.

There are two little things – reducing greed and negativity – which every person can and should work on in the daily decisions of their own lives in order to save the world. All people are responsible in some small way for our chaotic, deteriorating world. All are by nature selfish and self-centered and so the world has existed and evolved with a survival of the fittest impulse. This basic instinct / exercise or procedure / conduct / activity is both greedy and violent. Reducing greed and moving toward sharing more with others will benefit the whole world. Such mature activity will provide a caring mentality along with graceful living. The second goal of cutting down on negative thoughts, hurt-full aggression and destructive actions (violence) is equally important. As an individual moves toward complimenting others, building up the environment and co-operating / blending with all living things, all kinds of peaceful possibilities come into play. Obviously, each person can have an important role to play in this grand goal.

To end this discussion about what is important and maybe even necessary for human beings to act on in the great challenge of saving the world, here is a rather surprising suggestion. On this earth, death for some parts can mean new life for others. The simple illustration for earth-bound people is the example of a seed being deposited into the ground to die in order that much fruit can flourish. We all know about this scientific truth, but because of our immature and unnatural fear of death, we are very reluctant to see ourselves as the single, dying seed. Yet when we add in all the potential benefits that can be yielded in one person's life, that one dynamic, blessed spirit can honestly and factually produce lovely beauty and a sweet taste for eternity. Mature people in our world can look at death as a freeing up of the spirit to live in others, venturing on and on. Consider the motivation any person could have to make the most of one's precious days. The purpose would be to enhance the living of those around him or her as well as to benefit our entire planet's home and family. Being open to facing reality, looking at a world view, seeing what can be done to save something infinitely valuable, and envisioning oneself as an important part of the whole creation – this approach to life and living can be much more awesome, rewarding and joyful than trying to prepare oneself to live in dreamland. Be certain of this truth.

Religious Strengths

Doing our best to save the world, we all need to tap into the resources we have at our disposal. Since religions have played such a significant role in our lives, they undoubtedly can offer some insights for the future. Actually, there are quite a few good things that they have provided for the human race over the centuries. We can assume that they rose up out of the throws of history as essential for a growing civilization. Where would the human race have found its identity, value and potential without its inspiration from religions? The answer: There may well have been a reign of chaos. Individuals like Moses and Jesus (in the Christian religion) provided hope and meaning for desperate people in terrible turmoil. Look at Jesus for example: He wanted followers during his life-time, not worshipers. "Follow me", he said. Jesus was humble, sacrificial, loving, caring and very inspirational. He certainly wanted his followers to carry his spirit forward in their lives. Today, he is the primary Christian example. Other religions certainly have worthy leaders to follow.

Great people have provided enduring inspiration for countless followers over hundreds if not thousands of years. They have had their roots in even today's religions. So every generation needs its heroes and miracle workers to give direction and hope. Naturally, certain accounts of the words and activities of outstanding individuals have been magnified in memories, recitations and explanations to the point of being without historical content. However, that has not dimmed the enthusiasm of those looking for something special. Throughout the years, many less than reputable leaders have manipulated fuzzy accounts to grab the attention of those wanting to believe. That has given rise to what has been regarded as miraculous deeds and events interpreted as worthy of worship. With often a void in spiritual connections, weak and often ignorant members of social networks grab on to almost any religious thrilling story available. And so the story is passed on as though it is historical fact. Now that is not to discount the value of inspiring people in almost every generation who show others how to live with great exuberance and dedication. Today, almost every religion has its notable figures that are worthy of praise and even imitation. They may stand out as very special, but each one is merely another piece of a grand event called life, as worthy as they might be of leading and inspiring many. Religions can be viewed as having a treasure trove of admirable individuals who can even now grant us insights on how to live freely and victoriously. We need not reject or diminish precious words and actions of people from the past, whether they come from our immediate family or from long ago. We can use what they have offered us to build an even greater world view of having caring, creative communities everywhere.

As we look back in history to those lively, picturesque, emotional, inquisitive days, we see races, nations and communities captivated not only by personalities but also by religious stories and traditions. It enabled them to thrive and survive under very difficult circumstances. It gave them a focus for their lives, a kind of government for strength and security as well as a simple moral code for daily living. Religions, factions and movements were undoubtedly the talk of the town and rightly so. Religions and governments had their proper place for organizing, uniting and motivating their followers and citizens. There certainly was lively controversy as time flowed forward, but people could find identity and some meaning for their lives. Religions have provided moral guidelines as well as valuable direction and organization.

The basic moral foundations of most of today's cultures have been created by religions from the distant past. Those moral foundations are neither for nor against the morality of modern man. However, they can offer us a certain perspective on what seems to have worked over the years and what has caused us problems. What kind of morality is appropriate, instructive and practical in the world today? What do we need more of and what guidelines should be scrapped? Modern, maturing men and women need to find a way of life that takes into account all peoples and all forms of life. It might be helpful and encouraging for present day religious people to look to their best traditions and doctrines for contributions worthy of today's modern age. That kind of economic transition could enable considerable cooperation from all parts of the globe. A moral code that enables people to be free for the sake of creativity and responsible activities should be fundamental. Also, a moral code that could be flexible enough to change for the sake of needed new living standards should be developed. Morality can't be static where life and death matters are at stake. Furthermore, the living standards of the whole world are held in the balance when specific codes and laws are in place. Flexibility in suggested lifestyles for the sake of diversity and economy would be essential. In any case, the moral foundations of religions are worthy of study for trying to find a place to start.

The spirit of a person is vitally important to a good life on earth. Generally, many religious teachings have emphasized the spirit over the material world. This emphasis should not be continued in a new age of maturity, but it is still essential to keep the spirit in a prominent position related to the material world. Where would the world be headed if only material things were taken into account? The spirit has potential for development maybe even far beyond what is possible for physical change. Who is to know where the future will take us in the realm of the spirit? Sad to say, religions have pushed otherworldly life into human thinking so much that the physical things of this earth have been depreciated. This may be a major reason why living in a kind of fantasy land has been so attractive to people. Not only could they minimize or reject natural parts of earthly living but they could even demonize parts of creation along with their basic ways of functioning. This part of religious doctrine has probably been one of those add-on propositions put forward by less than wise and reputable leaders in order to enhance tall tales from the past. Since the things of the spirit are unseen and eternal life is not factually evident, it was not unexpected or strange that the connection between the unseen and eternal life was made and lifted to one of the most captivating stories of all time – a new life after death. How seductively it ties in with our human insecurity, ego and emotional makeup. All this being said, the realm of the spirit in human life is vital to the renewal of the earth and the advance of humanity's rational, factual, healthy, meaningful spot in the universe. What the eyes can see, our fingers touch, the ears hear and the tongue can taste is not all that we can experience in our existence. What is unseen is a very important part of life on this planet and human beings are truly blessed to possess spiritual insight.

Maybe one of the most beneficial aspects of what traditional religions have presented to people is the emphasis on giving, sharing and sacrifice. Most of the earth's inhabitants would consider this emphasis worthy of high praise. In fact, the advance of civilization can be attributed in large part to the demonstration of sacrifice in daily living. Caring, sharing and giving on this earth is what can make life beautiful, harmonious, thoughtful and enduring. Most people are awed by examples of people who have done unbelievable things for the sake of others. In fact, such examples have been so exalted in the minds of communities, races and nations that the demonstrations have been lifted up to be even worshiped. These concrete actions of some of the world's most outstanding individuals can never be erased from history. They truly have inspired untold benefits to all of earth's inhabitants. The life of sacrifice – not the actions of greed, plunder, aggression, competition and hate – is what the world needs now to move on to maturity, healing and health. It is our inheritance that people out of the past have shown each of us what can be done for the sake of a higher purpose – a goal of bringing opportunity, re-creation, splendor, cooperation and peace to our planet. It is worthy of being part of our future.

In a synopsis of what religions have contributed positively to life in the past, it shouldn't be neglected that they have provided people a feeling of hope. Hopefulness is critical for giving life. It's probably only a hopeful person who wants to continue to live, have children or do good deeds for others. Hope usually takes root in a positive environment and so is dependent on real, positive experiences. Most of us would not be hopeful based on simply our dreams, even pleasant ones. But in terrible times throughout history, when people saw light at the end of the tunnel, they usually experienced hope. Many religions were born out of bad situations for a group of people or for a nation. Then by means of a person or event, something awesome or extraordinary happened which gave them hope – what they needed desperately to survive. It's no wonder that recollections of those experiences were passed along generation after generation. One or more events may well have been the essential stimulus for positive living conditions. For any particular group of people, what a wonderful way out of continuing to dwell on a bad and sad state of affairs in daily living. There was hope. Jesus was one person in history that provided real hope to many around him.

The Historical Jesus

All major religions have their important historical leaders. Jesus is one of those historical figures. Such leaders have inspired many people to listen to their statements and to act on their suggestions. They have portions of their personalities and words often documented by dedicated followers and consequently, they are held in high regard and even worshiped by countless people throughout the ages. Some of these leaders have had a tremendous influence on the lives of their followers. They even have had a considerable life-style impact on individuals, communities and nations. These great leaders should not be cast aside simply because some of their followers have misunderstood or falsified their words. It would be natural that even certain important actions could have been misrepresented after their deaths. Still, their great contributions in history are worthy of remembering and applauding for the goodness and health of our lives even today.

The historical Jesus is one example of an impressive religious leader who has deeply influenced multitudes throughout the world for nearly 2,000 years. We should praise this great man for the inspirational life he laid out for the purpose of enhancing the life and health of people everywhere. It's true that the details of Jesus' life were simply made known for decades by means of oral tradition. There is almost no way to know exactly how Jesus lived moment by moment in his short life. Yet we can get a pretty good understanding of the impact he had on those who witnessed his words and deeds. The considerable impact is worth a lot to us as we look at our distressed world today and try to figure out how to save it. In fact, it would not be unreasonable to suggest that Jesus' whole life was dedicated to saving the world. It would be instructive to check out how his spirit was focused on giving the best of daily life to everyone. The following are some of the treasures he presents to us.

Jesus was a man who cared deeply about the well-being of every individual. Whether it was a prostitute, a wealthy man, a religious leader, a government official, a man with leprosy or an adoring female, Jesus had something helpful or beneficial to say or do for each one. What he said or did wasn't necessarily what was expected or even desired, but it was what he felt each one needed at the time. The contact with Jesus pointed them in the right direction – in essence, it showed them the way to grow up.

The historical Jesus was a common man with simple tastes. He was never married that we know of and he was on the move much of his life. There was plenty he had to say concerning the religious establishment of his day and their rules and regulations. Most of it was criticism. He had little time for the kinds of restrictions they laid on people. To those who crowded around him, he spoke about what was good and right and true. Known as the carpenter's son, Jesus was close to nature – comfortable on a boat or on a hillside. Jesus was the kind of person the world needs in every age. He urged his followers to carry on in his footsteps.

This Jesus – this man of great historical significance – was a humble person. If there is any one personality trait that modern man should adopt from this teacher and prophet it is humility. His disciples were in awe of his words and actions among the people, but one of his most memorable moments was when he assumed the role of a servant and washed their feet. Would there be any better demonstration for showing today's world how to live for others than that example? Proud, power hungry and spoiled children that we are (living in the first world), what an eye-opener for a chance to save the world.

Jesus went about saving the world in his own way. That involved saving its many and varied parts one by one. As thankful followers wanted to give him help and praise, he directed them to the needy. He said, "As you have done it for one of the least of these my brothers and sisters you have done it for me." He specifically called attention to those in prison, widows and orphans, the sick and helpless, the hungry and homeless as well as other groups of people belittled and rejected. Certainly these are the kinds of people hurt the most by the disasters of the world today. How important it is for people who hold Jesus in high regard to be about the business of making right what in the recent past has gone wrong. If we are in need of refreshing our minds about what should be done, the tasks have to do with seeking out a humble spirit, reducing what we want and need for daily living, caring about and for the needy of the world, deleting the big ego mentality of simply looking for personal salvation, working diligently for understanding and cooperation around the world, and finally trying to encourage everyone to get involved in preserving and refreshing our wonderful home on earth. That in fact is the birthright of every person on our planet. The spirit of Jesus cares for every part of us. In thanksgiving, we who claim to be his followers want his spirit in us to gain momentum and go on forever.

Maybe Jesus' most outstanding work can be found in his sacrifice. We already have noted the importance of sacrifice. Here was a common man who gave himself completely to those around him who were down and out. He did all he could for them with healing, taking their side, forgiving them, celebrating with them, feeding them and helping them to see everlasting things. Toward the end of his life, not so surprising, the crowds wanted more. They wanted lasting power, material security and another life after death. But this knowledgeable man knew that these childish desires were not what they needed. He essentially said, no promises. So they put him on a cross and killed him. That was the end of his physical work – his final sacrifice. He gave it his all and simply asked others to follow him.

Certainly there are people around the world who have worshiped Jesus as part of the Christian Church's Holy Trinity. In the Church's creeds he is regarded as the only Son of God the Father – the creator God. So how should Jesus be regarded in an era of science, historical fact and the search for truth? If there is no Santa Claus – no additional life promised after death – should the historical Jesus be disregarded as a fake or as a mere fantasy figure? The simple answer to that is no. As noted above, Jesus simply asked his disciples to follow – to walk in his footsteps – in a sense, to be a little Jesus in daily living. Obviously, we live in a different age and so it would be impossible to do exactly the same kinds of things he did 2,000 years ago. But there is no doubt that Jesus lived in history as a real man... saying real things to people, doing real things in his daily life and inspiring countless multitudes. Lives were changed because of him. The world has changed in many positive ways because of him and today his spirit could change the course of the world. Jesus could be one of the primary life givers to our desperate world on life support. The spirit that could bring that refreshment into reality today cannot simply come from people confessing, singing, saying or praying the right words. The Christian Church has carried out too much of that nonsense for centuries. It has been done in a spirit of worship instead of a spirit of dedication to his life and work. It has been a gigantic cop out! No, the way Jesus can come back to life today is when his followers decide to live their lives in his spirit of freedom, forgiveness, honesty, humbleness, thankfulness, truth, peace, hope and love. In living out such a dedicated life, his followers (the people who remember him in all his goodness) can provide a lot of what the world needs to survive today's critical situation. What an honor it should be to speak and act courageously in his name. The purpose would be not to earn a way to another fantasy life, but to be a part of the puzzle that would advance the world to a more wonderful, beautiful, peaceful, enjoyable place to live. That mission can be accomplished in the here and now.

How can Jesus – the great historical man of Palestine – bring about a new, creative, practical use of resources in this 21st century? One of the most concerning subjects for Jesus' admirers has to do with the structure of the Christian Church – not only the physical buildings and other assets but also the leadership and hierarchy throughout the world. What is to happen to all of that, especially since so many people of the past have contributed so much? In the first place, if in fact the resources (and people) have sincerely been dedicated to the work of Jesus Christ, certainly all this would joyfully be rededicated to his real work on earth today. Consider how the massive resources of the Christian Church could be used for the renewal of friendly relationships around the world, for helping people to cut back on unnecessary things in order to uplift and provide for the needs of others, and finally for helping people understand the importance of all living things in the creation. Consider the impact of all this on today's world, rather than have it focused on the mere worship of an imaginary god up in the sky somewhere. If the fact that there is no Santa Claus is truly understood by even most of the religious people of the world, the positives for earthly living would be mind-bogglingly. Everyone would be able to live much more enjoyable and satisfying lives. The even more satisfying consideration for this turnabout is that every living person could have a partnership in this Christ inspiring movement in the present – no worries for the future. What happens after death goes off into mystery. It would be clearly understood that the work of Jesus' spirit is a good, satisfying long term process meant to be a part of human living forever. This is good. Why not drop and forget the religious "Santa story"?

The historical Jesus is not diminished by cutting away

all the barnacles that have been amassed about him. As human beings, especially those who lived in an era of the Roman gods, it was in keeping with their times that an extraordinary human being should have special god-like powers. It was not so surprising that those who saw him in action and listened to his wonderful words would want him to be regarded above all others. The sad part is that human beings have little to contribute to knowledge about what is truly mysterious. The people who recounted the words and deeds of Jesus had no more knowledge about life after death than we do. They have had no more knowledge about Jesus' coming again than we do. They have had no more knowledge about the world coming to an end than we do. The only thing we know that they did not know is that the human species can in fact bring life as we know it to an end in the present. And tragedy above all tragedies, the reason is because we have disregarded Jesus' suggestions. Without all the barnacles, it really is crucial that Jesus' real spirit be brought back to life now.

Having had Christian connections in the past (I was a Lutheran minister for 14 years), I have had some deep ties to the Christian Church. Admittedly, I had some real questions about the structure of the Church toward the end. Before I left, I wrote an extensive paper entitled, "Should I Leave the Parish Ministry". Finally, I freely left the church in 1982 after serving in three parishes. I say this to admit that it has taken me some time to come to my present realization and offer these thoughts. In no way do I feel I have rejected the idea of a god or what may come after a person dies. I do not tremble about salvation or worry about eternity. In fact, I feel a sense of liberation in speaking out about what I believe. I believe I am speaking for the spirit of Jesus and doing what I can to (in a sense) raise him from the dead. He is still my leader, Master and Commander. As best I can, I am trying to reveal a way to move his life saving work out of the past into action in confronting the devastating situation on our planet. The man Jesus got it right. Jesus showed mankind the secret of living a full, rich abundant life.

I can't conclude a review of the historical Jesus without laying out some remarks for those who have been deeply involved with the Christian Church. I must suggest again that all is not lost in forgetting about Santa – forgetting about another life after death, salvation, eternal life. What is to know and what is lost in letting this go? Faith can be much stronger in the struggles of the real world we live in. We can act with freedom from the rules and regulations imposed by ancient men... as Jesus wanted. We can live in true love – caring about all others, humble, self-giving and sacrificial without reward. Furthermore, there is no competing, just yielding. You have to admit that is extraordinary love – special far beyond what most people experience these days. Doing this is to give thanks – to live a life of thanksgiving. There is contentment in living a blessed, forgiven, unique life in the friendship of Jesus. We are told that he called us his friends. He lived and died showing us the way to take part in his eternal spirit. There is no waiting for a blessed life. It's for the taking here and now.

Jesus is not the only outstanding religious leader. Other great religions of the world have certain men who have inspired countless people. Like Jesus, they deserve special recognition for what they have offered to the human race in their lives. But like Jesus, many of these profound speakers and actors on the world stage have had people misrepresent them as time moved on. Religions tend to often conform to very low standards when unethical people who want a cut of the power and profits squeeze in. Fantasies and fallacies are absorbed and carried forward, sometimes to places where the religion can hardly be recognized. This may well be the reason the religions of the world have been such a disaster in world history. It needs to be said that when a person like Donald Trump gains a foothold close to ignorant, childish, religious people, there can be terrible, terrifying consequences. Profound leaders from the past can be discredited and disgraced. So it goes on the child's playground of life. In such cases, it will require a lot of growing up to get the world back from facing a catastrophic ending.

Conclusion

The world has been headed towards disaster for quite a while now. These days we are beginning to recognize that fact. Our species – the most impact-full life form ever on the face of the earth – has been focused almost entirely on its own present survival. The most shocking aspect of this statement is that our species has been looking for that new way of living away from the earth! As wonderful, beautiful, valuable and durable as our planet has been for us, we look for some kind of escape from it. Sad to say, we as human beings have been the cause of our planet's systematic and overall decline. Thinking about the situation we are in and about who we are and what we are interested in, we need a big jolt of reality. We have been living fast and loose (at least the most consumptive portion of people on our planet) and we need something to set us straight. Who or what can do that? For most addicts (and we certainly are addicted to our present lifestyle or way of living), it traditionally takes an earth shaking crisis to get one to go for help. Obviously the people who should be knowledgeable about the world's condition have not experienced enough of a crisis to change course. The more ignorant and immature people of our world are in denial of our problems... or they want to escape from whatever bothers us. There's plenty to want to get away from on earth – ignorance, lack of caring, loss of memory, degenerative illnesses, sadness, depression, hopelessness, helplessness, fatalism and the list goes on. This is a very troubling situation because it means that we may not figure out what we are doing wrong in time to even save ourselves, say nothing about our earthly home. As the dominant remaining species on planet earth, do we even have what it takes to save the world?

If we could get our act together, who would benefit from the world being saved? There certainly would be plenty of motivation for proceeding with positive change since the whole world would benefit. Present and future generations could have some hope that the world's condition would improve. Any mysterious creative force or prime mover would be inspired. So what could be done to save the world? Even any small impacts by any small entities would begin to reverse the deterioration and destruction. They then might influence further creative actions. How could the saving be started? Small steps usually result in solid, good, lasting change so no efforts would be wasted. Where would inspiration come from? It would be important that any leadership for saving the world would come from dedicated and knowledgeable sources with good and proven accomplishments. That might originate from creative individuals, a religion, a source of moral teaching, an admired philosophy, etc.

Perfection as we humans understand the word does not have a place on our planet, and so we know mistakes would be made. That should only inspire more and better change as an ongoing adventure. Could an inspired human race actually improve the world from its jungle mentality or survival of the fittest philosophy? People united in moving toward gracious up-building for themselves and others would be the key to saving the world. Why shouldn't the peoples of the world have such potential for growth and development?

So what's going to shake us up to motivate us to change direction? We need to grow up... and getting some education is one answer. We definitely need to know what's going wrong as well as the part we play in the rapid deterioration. The steps needed are almost infinite, since all parts of life on earth are not only a part of the problem but also part of the solution. Of course, human beings have not only caused most of the problems but also play a necessary role in finding and instituting a solution. Religions have caused a great deal of disturbance in the world and have given us a very poor focus of attention. They have kept us in an immature, egocentric perspective concerning the world and our responsibilities in the world. Consequently, the way for us to grow out of this immaturity is for each person to analyze his or her own capabilities to become a truly mature creature. That may be all one can do, but it is a significant step in healing a broken and distressed planet. It will take time for the tide to turn toward finding and realizing a refreshed, harmonious, sustainable, fulfilling and happy place to live.

A major part of growing up is in realizing or taking account of what one can accomplish. That necessarily requires that each individual takes full responsibility for his or her priorities. To be sure, poor, egocentric, selfish priorities are literally destroying all we have on this earth. But who is willing to stick one's neck out to tell the truth to the rambunctious, irresponsible, greedy, egocentric, emotional offspring of our age? It's not easy, it carries certain consequences, and it may be totally disregarded until the cost becomes big enough. That's too bad for a world on life support. Will the understanding little people of the world have enough impact for bringing about change? Can the momentum be reversed? From the standpoint of watching newscasts of chaos around the globe, whether that news focuses on mass murders, lavish greed, unconscionable hunger, devastating weather, cutthroat competition, or manipulative government leaders paid off by big money – all this appalling news seems to leave us without much hope. The upside is that by far the majority of the earth's population wants and needs radical change. The priorities of these multitudes could probably rather quickly be oriented toward a more equal, cooperative, peaceful, caring, liberating, redeeming and harmonious world.

How can maturing individuals use their time, talents, resources and testimonials to essentially save the world? That challenge is a moment by moment exercise for human beings that is fundamental for the earth's well-being. Where knowledgeable people no longer need to or want to try to get themselves saved, they can now use what they have been given for a truly grand goal – bringing the earth back to life and health. This is a creative, artistic project each person can have a share in developing (no matter how large or small the action) over a full life-time. This is not an unreal dreamed up life of desired rewards or benefits in the future. On the contrary, it is a life each human being can realistically control in the present and that will be able to be documented by historical facts in the future.

One thing that will not be praised in a world of concrete facts and cooperative harmony is the kind of personal, self-adoration that is presently so common among those with tremendously big egos in our day and age. These individuals have tried to tie themselves and their accomplishments to god and his special goodness to them – as though their god has already given them a special place here and now. Where this kind of thinking has given our contemporaries the feeling that there are people who are better and more talented than others (like children playing games), in a more advanced and developed age, the inhabitants of our world will try to accommodate and uplift not only members of their own species but also the rest of creation. Around this new world, all forms of life will seek to be in harmony for the beauty and benefit of all. Right now, around the world in a religious, competitive and self-centered atmosphere, the witness to the universe is that we live in an age of the survival of the fittest. This isn't much of a change from the basic animal instincts of the distant past. Today, the new reality is that such past historical skills (where the big, powerful, wise and talented win out) are surely doomed to fail. Our species has affected life on earth so much (dominating and destroying) that even our very sources of life are disintegrating little by little. Daily living for most people is increasingly difficult and unfortunate. A radical change is needed as soon as possible.

All this being said, it's essential to put forward that mystery is a part of man's reality on earth and probably always will be. What that mystery entails is obviously beyond us. Whether we wonder about infinity, eternity, creation, god, or whatever, there is little reason to claim much knowledge. People can believe any number of things and certain beliefs can be beneficial for a meaningful, productive and blessed life. On the other hand, it's in our interest concerning the very survival of our planet that some beliefs have been and are a definite detriment to our lives. It would be valuable and important to distinguish what these beliefs are and try to move them out of our attention. Very basically, anything without historical fact or contrary to today's understanding of truth should be cleared away. What's left might well be worthwhile for interpersonal relationships in the future. In this analysis, it should not be stated that there is no god or that religions serve no purpose in the real world. It is important for every person to believe in something good, true and enduring. Throughout the ages, religions have documented what human beings have found profound in their experience. That documentation is worth remembering and preserving.

What has been covered in this discussion boils down to a mature point of view versus an immature one. As better educated human beings, it seems vital for all of us to encourage earth's inhabitants to take on more mature living in the present and future. This would involve caring for others versus just caring for oneself, peace versus violence, cooperation versus aggression, self-giving versus greed, generosity versus selfishness and kindness versus brutality. Who wouldn't want to share and promote these positives for daily living? In the end, today we desperately need good emergency care for all living things on earth. Everyone can help. Let's urge one-another to do away with living a fantasy, immature, egocentric and me-first life. There's a better way to live. It's in striving for humble, self-giving maturity. Let's get involved in saving the world!

T. Hans Olson